CONFESSIONS
OF A
TOTALED WOMAN

Also by Karen Wise:
God Knows I Won't Be Fat Again

CONFESSIONS
OF A
TOTALED WOMAN

Karen Wise

Thomas Nelson Publishers
Nashville

Publisher's Note: It seems not even authors should be expected to write *words* every time they face a blank sheet of paper. Although she fails to "confess" it in the pages that follow, Karen Wise is a doodler, and the doodle-art in this book is hers.

All rights reserved under International and Pan-American Conventions. Published in Nashville, Tennessee, by Thomas Nelson Inc., Publishers and simultaneously in Don Mills, Ontario, by Thomas Nelson & Sons (Canada) Limited. Manufactured in the United States of America.

All Old Testament Scripture quotations, unless otherwise indicated, in this publication are from the *King James Version* of the Bible.

All New Testament Scripture quotations, unless otherwise indicated, in this publication are from *The New King James Bible*-New Testament. Copyright © 1979, Thomas Nelson, Inc., Publishers.

Verses marked TLB are from *The Living Bible* (Wheaton, Ill.: Tyndale House Publishers, 1971) and are used by permission.

Library of Congress Cataloging in Publication Data

Wise, Karen.
   Confessions of a totaled woman.

   1. Christian life—1960-
2. Wise, Karen. I. Title.
BV4501.2.W574   248.4   80-10980
ISBN 0-8407-5725-5

Contents

Chapter 1

Help Stomp Out
Spiritual Giants

From my position behind the huge split-leaf
philodendron in the corner of the hotel lobby, I could
see her coming. She was the personification of the
total woman—every hair in place, beautifully dressed,
moving with grace and charm, a smile on her perfectly formed lips. Heads turned as she passed by, but
she moved on as if she were totally oblivious to the
admiring stares.

She was a few minutes late—delayed, I'm sure, by
ten important calls, all requesting her help or advice.

I could tell at a glance that she had experienced
another perfect morning. Mine had included an
eight-year-old with a bad disposition, a ten-year-old
with nothing to wear, and a run in my last pair of
pantyhose.

As she walked briskly across the marble lobby
floor, she was intercepted by an old acquaintance.
She chatted only briefly, just long enough to give a
man from the housekeeping department time to
finish watering and misting the plants.

Now, through the blur created by hair spray and

mascara running into my eyes, I watched her every move. As she came in my direction, I held my breath so there wouldn't be a breeze. She slowly passed the philodendron and headed down the stairs to the luncheon, to which both of us had been invited.

Waiting until she was out of sight, I slid from my temporary refuge, tried to fluff the damp bow at the neck of my blouse, shook the peat moss from my hemline, and forced myself toward the stairway. I felt like a clod as I clunked my way to the dining room, hoping we wouldn't be seated at the same table. It would be an altogether obvious case of the *total woman* versus the *totaled woman*.

Fortunately, my place card was halfway across the room from hers, and as I took my place I began to feel a little better about my chances of getting through the day in one piece.

For you see, I had found out through prior personal experience that this woman was a "spiritual giant." I don't use the term in a complimentary manner; it is the expression I use to describe Christian people who do not bother to get to know you, never invite you to their homes, never include you in any activities, are rarely sensitive to your needs, but somehow feel they know God's total will for your life. Without the slightest understanding of you or your circumstances, they seize on every opportunity to assess your weaknesses, tell you how to correct them, and show you an underlined Scripture verse from their well-worn, pulpit-sized Bibles.

They are people you can never look *at* on your level but always must look *up to*—not because they are necessarily examples you want to follow, but because they have an uncanny way of making you feel like a spiritual midget. It's spiritual intimidation!

Over the years I have met a number of these "spiritual giants," and even though I have never really hidden in the bushes to avoid them, I have wanted to.

In addition to what they seemingly consider their divinely appointed task of reconstructing your life to their specifications, they never miss the opportunity to leave you with the impression that, having arrived at such a high plateau, they no longer have problems, bad attitudes, or any need for improvement.

And to that, this wife and mother—this "totaled woman"—cannot relate!

I desperately need the continuing power and counsel of God in my life. I also benefit from friends who help me see my mistakes, who wrap their arms around me during the hard times, and who rejoice with me when my faith grows. I appreciate teachers and pastors who help me to more effectively apply God's Word to my daily activities, my attitudes, and my personal relationships.

If you look through the Bible, you will notice that God didn't use giants (except for Goliath, and he was on the side of the opposition!). Instead, He used Moses, David, Abraham, Sarah, Peter, Paul, Lydia, Thomas, and a couple named Mary and Joseph. They were all just regular-sized people.

Granted, the power of God was with them. He demanded a great deal from them, and He did supernatural things through them. But they were people who walked the streets of their cities and appeared to be just like everyone else. They laughed,

God. . . Sometimes I feel I'm bent the wrong way.

they cried, and some even found it a struggle to forsake all and follow Christ, even as He stood before them in the flesh.

But they were able to understand the struggles of others who were asked to follow Someone they had never seen. Do you think Thomas was qualified to understand the friend who admitted he was doubting his faith? Could Peter identify with the individual who was running scared? Did Paul look down upon his Jewish contemporaries?

Our contrasting personalities are useable in God's plan. He does not expect us to conform to the exact likeness of anyone else, even though other people may have qualities that are desirable and worthy of developing. God does not want any of us to be carbon copies of someone else. We are original creations, and He wants us to freely give expression to that which makes us who we are.

And you know what? God has never loved anyone any more than He loves me! I need to know that when I feel "totaled." Of course, He has never loved anyone else any less, either! The point is that *each of us is loved; each of us can be used.*

I want to be used. I don't always act like it, and there are days when I feel as if I haven't allowed Him to do much through me. But I know He has a unique place for me, and He develops my potential and gives me opportunities to use it for His purposes. And I don't have to be perfect.

A former persecutor of the church, a man small in stature, once wrote: "I have been crucified with Christ; it is no longer I who live, but Christ lives in me; and the life which I now live in the flesh I live by faith in the Son of God, who loved me and gave Himself for me" (Gal. 2:20).

When I weighed 345 pounds, I used to joke that if I had been nine feet tall I would not have had a problem. But I never wanted to be a physical giant any more than I wanted to be fat.

I don't want to be a spiritual giant either, not if I must give the impression of being a total woman on the outside. I want others to be able to look into my eyes, not at my waistline. You need to know that I've experienced all that goes into being a totaled woman—pain, rejection, loneliness, lack of faith, depression, and multiple broken spiritual noses from falling on my face. But I also want you to understand that I am experiencing forgiveness, peace, purpose, and an ability to face life through the redeeming love and unlimited power of Jesus Christ.

I want to share with you the progress God is bringing about in my life, as well as the areas where I am still having difficulties. This book is about those big areas of my life where I know I ought to practice what I say I believe.

Many times my struggles have seemed twelve feet tall, and the list of improvements I need to make longer than my grocery list and far more expensive. My problems are usually not very glamorous. They simply represent parts of my life that have been hard to turn over to the One who is big enough to handle them.

I dedicate this book to those who always end up choosing the slowest line in the grocery store or the bank. It's for those who get irritated with the guy who doesn't use his turn signal, but exhibits six religious bumper stickers for you to read while you're waiting for him to go left.

These confessions of a totaled woman are for husbands who wish they could cry and for wives who wish they could stop; for dads who are trading in their big cars and for mothers whose minds have been totally blown by the price of children's tennis shoes. These pages are for all of us who tend to let the "nitty gritty" of life get under our fingernails and into our hair.

I hope you laugh and cry and, most of all, identify with my personal experiences as I share them one by one. Living requires a daily dose of God-given wisdom, common sense, and understanding. Here's a good place to start:

> For the reverence and fear of God are
> basic to all wisdom. Knowing God results
> in every other kind of understanding
> (Prov. 9:10, TLB).

Chapter 2

I Live Through Crises— It's the Daily Hassles That Kill Me!

It's about 5:30 in the morning. I have already thanked the Lord for my coffeepot that clicks on automatically in preparation for my early arrival.

I've turned up the heat, felt my way to the kitchen light, and added "Sweet 'n Low" and two percent milk to the hot coffee in my favorite mug.

Now, with both hands wrapped around the warmth of the cup, I'm sitting here in all my splendor and glory.

My pajama bottoms and the huge green sweat shirt I wore to bed to cooperate with energy conservation display everything the "totaled woman" stands for. My bowling socks, sticking out from the top of my Indian moccasins, accessorize the outfit with a needed touch of sophistication.

My bland face, with none of the "distinct features" that will be created later in the day, is highlighted only by a slight smudge of mascara under each eye—dark spots not totally eradicated by the cold cream of the night before.

This picture of beauty is appropriately framed by

my hair, which resembles no style at all . . . but at least carries out a consistency in its overall look.

But who cares? There's not a soul in this room but me, and it's quiet and uninterrupted. Larry and the kids are still asleep, paying unconscious homage to the one part of the day I can call my own. The sun is also keeping the covers pulled up over its face, delaying the pitter-patter of little feet.

Believe it or not, after being a night owl all of my life, I've come to love the early morning. This is the time I keep to pray, to read, and to turn the wheels of my mind toward the coming activities of the day.

I seem to be so organized during this special time. My mind is creative and energetic. The day looks well planned; the ideas come fast; there don't seem to be any hurdles that can't be jumped. What I need to do to improve myself seems crystal clear, and my determination to be a wonderful wife and mother seems strong enough to withstand any problem that might intrude.

I just wish the superb grip on life that I have between 5:30 and 7:00 A.M. wasn't so easily blown to smithereens by a simple "I don't want to wear that dumb blouse!" hurled at me at 7:06. How easily my wonderful early morning personality goes up in smoke!

One needs only to look at my medicine cabinet to know how fortunate I am. The jar of cold cream, twelve varieties of nail polish, deodorant, and one small bottle of children's aspirin remind me that neither Larry nor the children have ever really been sick.

There have been no fractured bones, no allergies, and no colds that have lingered more than a week.

There's a roof over our heads, food on the shelves, clean clothes in the closets, and my husband is sleeping in *my* bed. The kids like school, the furniture is in good shape, the dishwasher works, and we haven't had any car repairs in two weeks.

When I take inventory, I have so much to be thankful for . . . so many blessings to count.

But I must admit that I have a tendency to allow all the terrific things in my life to be pushed out of sight and out of mind by a slight dose of the whines from my eight-year-old or a burst of terror from my daughter when she discovers she did her homework wrong last night.

You would think I'd have learned by now that the same God who saved me, healed and restored my marriage, and gave me strength to lose 210 pounds is also capable of handling my daily disposition and my moment-to-moment temperature gauge.

But like a lot of Christians I know, I seem to handle crises much better than life's daily hassles.

I find it much easier to hand over to Christ the desperate situations, the urgent needs, than I do the everyday, nitty-gritty things that I keep telling myself "any idiot should be able to handle."

And alas, *it's those small things that keep messing everything up!*

I don't worry as much about breaking my leg as I do about stumbling over some petty argument and falling flat on my face from losing my cool.

Most of us tend to think that those who come through crises—serious illness, total financial loss, the death of a loved one—victoriously in Christ are the epitome of godly people . . . and I'm not minimizing the meaning of those experiences. But the older I get, the more I appreciate the deep spiritual commitment of those who consistently remain victorious on a day-to-day basis, allowing Christ to shine through the routine of their businesses, their friendships, their relationships with their families, and another basket of dirty laundry.

To me, they are the real winners.

I have done much thinking in the past year about how badly I react to the little things, about how out of balance I let my joy and irritation become, about how often I let a day full of potential blessing appear dismal just because the kids forgot to brush their teeth again.

You see, by nature I'm the kind of person who would rather change the world than the beds. I would rather cook a gourmet meal than come up with one more way to fix macaroni. And I would much rather think up an idea than carry it out.

But I'm learning. And I'm finally asking for help from the Lord who loves me. I'm discovering in a new way that my nature is not Christlike unless I do things His way. For one thing, Christ is not selfish. *I am.* Selfishness makes me the most important person and amplifies every little thing that interferes with Number One.

It's always easier to *quote* Scripture verses than to *apply* them. I can't even remember how long ago I learned this one: "Delight thyself also in the Lord; and he shall give thee the desires of thine heart" (Ps. 37:4).

And then there is the prescribed antidote for daily hassle and irritation:

Rejoice in the Lord always. Again I will say,

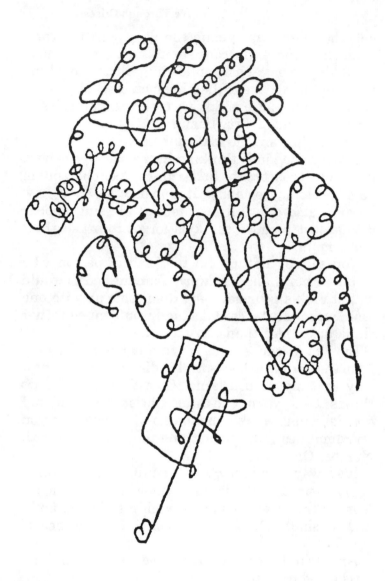

I'm up tight.

rejoice! Let your gentleness be known to all men. The Lord is at hand. Be anxious for nothing, but in everything by prayer and supplication, with thanksgiving, let your requests be made known to God; and the peace of God, which surpasses all understanding, will guard your hearts and minds through Christ Jesus" (Phil. 4:4–7).

The longest distance in the world seems to be that between my knowledge and my actions.

I ask myself so many times why after ten and a half years my kids can't remember that soap is essential to cleanliness or that the rug outside the door is there for a reason.

But sometimes my memory is no better. After thirty-six years there are still times when I forget that God understands me and wants to help me handle the little things.

When I don't forget, I grow by leaps and bounds.

Let me give you a couple of examples of how the Lord is helping me cope with the Monday-through-Sunday stuff.

I've always prided myself on being very organized, very neat, very color-coordinated, and very punctual. No wonder little things blow me to pieces! I used to feel it was unforgivable to go to bed with a dish in the sink. I would break out in a rash if someone put a pink towel in the blue stack or put a pair of socks on the undershirt pile. My stomach would be in knots if it were time to leave the house and my husband was still putting on his shoes. And I lost all composure if one of the kids appeared in a shirt and slacks that didn't match.

I still feel that being punctual and organized are

admirable qualities, but I know now that I selfishly let them get out of hand. My family wasn't really free to live in our house. They seldom made a mess because they knew I didn't like it. I'm sure that sometimes they were the ones with knots in their stomachs—just from living with me.

When I admitted that I was actually forcing my family to live with all *my* rules (good and bad), to assume *my* priorities, develop *my* tastes, and tiptoe through *my* domain, I also admitted how selfish I was.

As a wife and mother, I do believe in discipline, advice, guidance, and love; but I no longer believe I should try to clone "little Karens" out of those whom God so uniquely created.

I'm not perfect, anyway! And God, with His mighty, gentle chisel, is making changes in my life that (isn't it strange!) seem to smooth out everyone around me.

I now see that I made every little thing such an issue that it grew way out of proportion, and the slightest nudge felt like total disaster. That person who reacts negatively to every little thing, who makes a major point out of every minor detail, stays irritated most of the time. That ideal verse—"This is the day which the Lord hath made; we will rejoice and be glad in it" (Ps. 118:24)—lasts only until the first glass of spilled milk.

Well, I for one don't plan to live that way anymore. And my family isn't going to bunk with an irritable prune, either. I have asked the Lord to give me the ability to make issues only of the important, to reprimand only when necessary, to deal with problems in a firm but loving voice, and to view the insignificant as just that.

More importantly, I pray daily that I will display more happiness than irritation, and more appreciation than disapproval.

After all, that's the way I want to be treated!

One of the practical steps I've taken is backward. I am starting to delay my reactions when I'm irritated until I can step back and ask myself these questions:

1. Am I irritated over something important?
2. Is it going to make any difference this time tomorrow?
3. Am I fighting for an insensitive, personal opinion or a principle of life upon which God puts great importance?
4. Is my method of handling the problem going to wipe out the value of my correction?

I still blow it from time to time, but I pleasantly am aware of the changes that are taking place.

My husband and our little boy now work jigsaw puzzles on the dining room table for days at a time, with hardly a murmur from the former chairman of the "Keep-Our-Dining-Room-Spotless" committee.

My ten-year-old daughter actually has posters on her wall that don't match her bedspread. And my husband, free at last, openly piles books and magazines on the floor by the bed without wondering when the nagging boom will fall.

My home is still neat, but we're enjoying each other more because I've relaxed on insignificant things.

I am also working on another little project that a

friend passed on to me a few weeks ago. I share it here, hoping it will be of help to you.

This project is called "positive first." Whenever any member of my family walks in the door after school, work, sports, or other activities, I am disciplining myself to make my first statements to that person positive ones.

Now some days this is very difficult, believe me. When the door flies open, my kid is standing there with a hole in the knee of his pants, school spaghetti sauce smeared down the front of his T-shirt, and his first words are, "I'm so mad at John I'll never speak to him again," I've got to be very creative.

I could ask, "Did you have a good day?" But somehow, under the circumstances, that wouldn't seem positive. I'm afraid to ask where his jacket is, or if he brought home a library book, because my gut instinct says, "Those questions wouldn't strike a positive chord either."

So sometimes I simply say, "You left your room very neat this morning. I really appreciate that." Or, "I was thinking what you might like for a snack when you got home, and I made some custard because I know it's your favorite."

I can't guarantee you that two positive statements will turn members of your family into loving, giving, uncomplaining people. But you'll be surprised what it will do for you. Your attitude will be different, I promise.

Now let me tell you about my twelve-year marriage, to which I am still adjusting daily.

When my husband and I got together, I don't think you could have found two more opposite people. After eleven years, we're not opposite any more—we're just different! That's all right, because if I had married someone just like me, we would have killed each other by now. If Larry had married someone like him, they wouldn't be able to get around in the house because of the stuff they would have collected.

I should have smelled the rat of contrast when he showed up at our wedding rehearsal in old slacks and a cardigan sweater. It looked slightly out of step with my cocktail dress and dangling earrings. Boy, did I react. I didn't speak to him again until I said "I do" twenty-four hours later!

Larry brought with him to our newly formed nest a truck full of antique furniture and a collection of four hundred owls. I brought a wardrobe and a few boxes of old music and scripts. I hated that old stuff he brought, but I must admit his contribution was a lot more comfortable to sit on. And today we still have that furniture, and more of it. And the wonder of it is that I've really come to like it! (The four hundred owls, however, have multiplied to more than eight hundred; and I feel I could be close to my maximum owl capacity.)

Larry likes old cars. I like new ones that run. He likes flea markets. I like the theatre. He likes dead-end streets and "shortcuts." I like expressways and the assurance that we will arrive at our destination. Larry knows north from south. I confuse right with left. He cuts out coupons and throws them away when they expire. I don't bother.

One of Larry's habits, in particular, always has been a source of great irritation to me. *He saves everything.* Now when you understand that I am a "throw-it-away" fanatic, you can see why that could create some conflict. In addition to antique furniture and owls, he also collects antique books and magazines of every vintage. We have every issue of some publications—and no storage space. If our bed broke, we wouldn't drop an inch!

Every time there is a historic event or disaster, we have to have two untouched copies of the newspaper to save for the children. (I surely hope they appreciate them!) I am so used to it that when I heard Teng Hsiao-ping was scheduled to come to Atlanta, my first thought was: "Oh, no—two more newspapers!" Add to that the four or five daily papers on the floor by the bed and every good paper the kids have ever brought home from school—and you have one heavy house.

There are piles on the closet shelves, books in every drawer, boxes in storage, and always a stack we can't put away because he hasn't looked through it yet.

There's nothing more exciting than an enthusiastic voice saying, "Karen, guess what? This book was written in 1903, and it still has the dust jacket!" Now, I know I should respond with a "Does it really?" as I drop everything and run to view the newest addition to our valuable clutter. But for years my unspoken reaction has been, "I wish he'd pay half as much attention to me as he does to those dingy old books."

And then one day I stopped to wonder if perhaps he had thought the same thing when I was engrossed in a musical production or overbearingly excited about another outrageous dream.

I am becoming more convinced every day that the quality of life, marriage, children, and vocation depends on how we handle the little things—the details, the responses, the words, the attitudes.

We often hear people say that a crisis pulled a family together. But how many times do we admit that it was the everydayness of life, poorly handled, that created the crisis?

Instead of resting in the knowledge that God knows our needs and focusing on the fact that He promises to meet them, we alone try to force every activity and relationship in the direction of fulfilling those needs. That's where we get into trouble.

You know what still really irritates me? Finding the same clothes in the laundry three times a week when I've spent a lot of money on a whole closet full of clothes that are never worn. Watching my husband turn out lights behind me to save energy when he will drive to six different stores to find something we don't really need. Putting two coats of wax on the kitchen floor and realizing no one cares.

Yes, I've got a long way to go. And if I'm not careful, I can let these kinds of things affect everything I do.

When we put all our energy into human remedies for little things that go against our grain, we don't develop our God-given resources that enable us to appreciate all the wonderful things He has done for us.

Zero in on the goodness of God and see what happens to your attitude.

Pray consistently for a daily dose of the joy of the Lord and see if your children become less irritating.

Focus on developing your maximum potential for God and see if the pile of magazines gets only an occasional glance.

It works!

And when I apply these things in my life, you know what I discover?

That my children are a joy more often than an irritation.

That people make more right moves than mistakes.

And that my husband is far more knowledgeable than I am . . . because he reads a lot. I am beginning to appreciate his knowledge, his interests, his contribution to a conversation, and the value of all those piles and hobbies.

And I am learning that God knew my needs all along.

"Thank you, Lord, for teaching me this lesson. May I continue to learn it every day. And please help Larry adjust to the fact that I dispose of bottle caps in drawers instead of in trash cans, that I'd like to move the furniture over and over again, that I have to have all three hundred pictures hung the first day in a new house, and that I've thrown away some things I wish I had kept."

Chapter 3

Whatever Happened To the Belly Laugh?

Once in a while, when I was a little girl, I used to sneak out of bed, tiptoe to the top of the stairs, and sit on the top step, bent over so that my nightgown would be long enough to keep my toes warm.

The main attraction was the continual laughter that originated in the living room but literally filled the whole house. It sounded like everybody was having such a good time I couldn't stand missing out on all the fun.

My folks didn't see their close friends often because most of them traveled, but when they did get together it seemed as though they laughed for hours. One would tell a story, then another, and soon it didn't make any difference who said what. Everything was funny!

When they got to that point you never heard a slight chuckle or a sophisticated "ha, ha, ha." What you got, folks, were pure, unadulterated belly laughs . . . the kind that make your sides hurt and tears run down your face, the kind that make you beg for a break just to get your breath.

From my spot on the stairs, I would watch and

listen and say to myself, "I can hardly wait till I grow up and I can do that."

Well, I'm all grown up now; in fact, I have been for quite some time. And I want to know: Whatever happened to the belly laugh?

I love to laugh, and I admit it unashamedly. I feel terrific when I have laughed from the soles of my feet and my blush is dripping from my chin.

But lately, I feel like my belly-laugh reservoir is becoming stagnant. Worse than that, I feel that some of that uncontrollable hysteria-in-waiting is inwardly being broken down and rationed out as mere giggles. And it's just not the same thing.

About ten years ago, the Christian world was hit by the concept of sharing. We were urged from every side to care for one another—to bear one another's burdens. Share groups for every age sprang up across the country. Agape love became an interdenominational term, and for the first time, many of us began to understand it.

It gave thousands of Christians their first opportunity to talk about their problems without a condemning response. The term "fellowship of believers" took on renewed meaning, and many churches were prompted to be more open and practical in meeting people's real needs.

I agree we needed it, and we still do. It is just that now I occasionally feel I have an entire telephone book full of people who want to share my pain, and a very short list of those who want to laugh with me. I am of the strong opinion that a good sense of humor and the ability to laugh and have a good time are vital parts of the lives God has given us.

There have been many times down through the

years when I have been very grateful to God for the ability to laugh. Those light moments were often just the break I needed to change my perspective—to realize that all was not dark, but under the direction of God Himself.

There have been days that seemed to be full of problems, when I found the person who dropped in just to lighten my mood more sensitive than the one who begged me to share my innermost feelings.

Just as I know it is healthy to have someone to talk to, I feel it can be unhealthy to talk continually about problems—ours and everyone else's.

Granted, it seems that everywhere you look people are in trouble today. If it's not their finances, it's their marriage. If it's not their marriage, then it's their children. If it's not their children, it's their self-esteem, and on it goes. I understand—believe me, I've had them all. And I've done my share of talking, griping, and crying. But when I dwell on my own problems and then listen to everyone else's, I've got to have a change of pace once in a while. Otherwise, I begin to look, feel, and (worse) act like a dealer in secondhand blues and discount depression.

It's amazing how many Christians tell you they have turned their problems over to the Lord, and then remind you of each one in detail every time you see them. They always end the conversation with, "But I know God will take care of everything. I'm trusting Him."

I'm not trying to recommend that we hide from our problems or run away from the realities of life. All I'm recommending is that we hang on to the joy, remind ourselves we can laugh, and find the hours to simply have a good time.

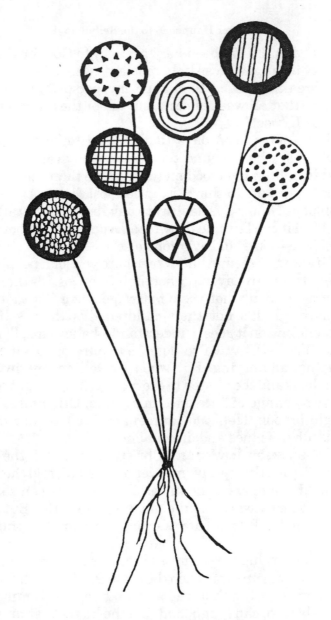

You've got to let go occasionally.

I earnestly desire to be more compassionate, more understanding, and more sensitive to the needs of others. And I feel that the hours I take to step back, enjoy being alive, giggle at myself, and act a little crazy are invaluable to my Christian life. Those times are like a breath of fresh air, giving me a better attitude to face what's ahead.

We don't hesitate to ask God to help us use and develop the other qualities He intended us to have; why not ask Him to give us a renewed feeling of enjoyment and the great emotional release of deep-down laughter?

Then was our mouth filled with laughter, and our tongue with singing: then said they among the heathen, The Lord hath done great things for them (Ps. 126:2).

Do you believe He does great things? Convince me. Don't become stuffy, somber, and preoccupied with your problems and the troubles of those around you. Dare to laugh a little!

Whatever happened to those nights when friends kicked off their shoes and sat around singing all the dumb songs they learned at camp years ago? Whatever happened to the times you stood with someone in a parking lot for an hour and laughed after everyone else had gone home? What about those committee meetings that used to end with nothing accomplished because no one could be serious? Weren't they fun?

How long has it been since you were at a party where everyone went bananas and told all the funny things that happened in college or at their wedding?

You know what I think? I think the belly laugh got

thrown out with spontaneity! We are so tightly scheduled, so well-planned, so wrapped in calendars that we have even tried to assign our laughter and fun to a certain slot. It just doesn't work that way, so in many cases we have eliminated it.

Think back. Many of the memorable times in your life were probably times that just "happened."

Oh, I realize you may own your own business, and you probably have children with soccer games and choir practice. I know about the four boards you are on and the big house you have to keep up. But there has to be a moment of pressure lapse when you say, "That's it; I've got to laugh . . . now!"

The best times are spur-of-the-moment kind of times. We've forgotten that, or at least we've chosen to live without it. Whoever told us that maturity should wipe out our desire for plain old fun should think again.

When my kids were tiny, we used to all climb in our big bed, sing action choruses, giggle, and tell funny stories. Eight years later they still come to me every once in a while on a cold night and say, "Let's put our pajamas on and crawl into your bed and laugh." They don't remember the thirty-dollar toys they had when they were two and three years old. They don't remember that we spent extra money to make sure they had a good time at Disneyland. But they do remember there was something special about laughing together.

The kind of laughter and fun I miss is the kind that doesn't cost any money. At the most, it will put you out the expense of a jug of cider, a bowl of popcorn, and some wonderful moments of your time.

It isn't unspiritual to laugh. Just because you

spend a marvelous, fun-filled evening with your friends doesn't mean you don't care about a dying world or your neighbors who are facing divorce. Some of the most godly, caring, sensitive people I know can laugh louder than anyone else.

I believe God intended for us to experience joy as much as anything else. He gave us the gift of laughter. He created a sense of humor and put it within us, right alongside our ability to cry and hurt and sympathize.

Treat your kids to living proof that you don't have to drink or get high on drugs to have a terrific time. Your example of the Christian's capacity for fun and laughter will stand strong when your teen-ager begins to compare you with other parents on the block.

Give your husband or wife the opportunity to hear about the dumb mistake you made today. If it wasn't funny when it happened, it could be hilarious a few hours later.

And if you are a little down, covered up with everybody's problems, if there are eighty-five people all in crises on your prayer list, if every telephone call brings another person wanting you to share their burdens, maybe you need to ask the Lord to help you find a joy break in your day.

For a change, pray today about joyful things. Thank the Lord for music. Tell Him how happy you are you have a washer and dryer. Thank Him for allowing you to find your new pair of $35.00 shoes on sale for only $15.99. When you've given thanks for the good things you have, then do some spur-of-the-moment things.

Why not dress up on Halloween, make a giant

pumpkin cookie, and drop in on your neighbor? Why not run through the sprinkler with your kids? Afraid you might get wet? You'll dry off, and everybody will have a good time.

Make a dozen caramel apples and put them on a cookie sheet. Walk halfway to school to meet your kids and let them treat their friends.

Call your husband and tell him you're packing a picnic supper and you and the kids will meet him on the front steps of City Hall. When he points out that it's only thirty degrees outside, tell him you're part of a survey to find out how long "take-out" chicken stays warm in freezing weather, and you will bring his heavy coat. I guarantee that while you're eating you will either laugh a lot or freeze to death with a drumstick in your mouth.

If you're not that crazy, at least pick up the phone, call a friend, and say, "I feel like laughing." Know what kind of response you will probably get? "You know, I feel like laughing, too. It's been so long since I've had a good laugh."

From now on, don't pass up those opportunities to get together with old friends at the last minute, to roll on the family-room floor with your kids, or to surprise your neighbors by appearing on their doorstep at midnight with a yogurt milkshake.

Having fun won't detract from your involvement in the needs of others. It won't keep you from having a ministry or studying the Word of God. It will enhance your life, improve your attitude, and give you the healthy break we all need.

I think the Lord knew we would sometimes get too close to our problems, making them seem fuzzy and out of proportion. I think He knew we would have a tendency to so clutter our minds that we would need to sift through everything and start our understanding process all over again. And for those times He gave us the precious gift of a sense of humor.

I intend to use it. So if you are sitting in a restaurant someday and you hear a genuine belly laugh—the kind that comes from deep within and spreads to everyone else around—you'd better turn around and look.

It just might be me. And I'd hate for you to miss out on the fun.

Chapter 4

A Paper Plate Will Do

I sat down beside a lady at a church dinner recently, and during the course of the conversation she said, "We just have to get together for coffee one of these days. I've been so busy, but my schedule is just bound to lighten up soon and then we'll get together. I'll give you a call." I nodded and the conversation went on.

Just because I didn't respond verbally doesn't mean I wasn't interested. In fact, I would have enjoyed getting together with her. It's just that for over a year she has said that same thing to me every time she has seen me.

At this point, I've decided that either she doesn't want to get together at all, or she's waiting for a domestic miracle. She's probably looking for the clear day on her calendar that coincides with the same time the kids are at Grandmother's, and the maid just happens to leave two fruit cups, two cheese danish, and two cups of hot tea sitting on the counter. In other words, I feel my chances of wrapping my hands around one of her mugs are very slim.

Then there are the people who say, "I'd love to have you and your husband over, but I can't entertain like you do." Add to those the people who never invite anyone over unless every particle of dust has been eliminated. Multiply by those who have to plan everything four weeks in advance and never know when their husbands are going to be out of town. Squeeze in those who have never entertained and aren't willing to try, and those who feel their homes aren't impressive enough—and you have thousands of people who are missing out on a terrific part of life!

Can I ask you something? What do you do with your home besides clean it? Has it become only an in-and-out station for your family and a couple of neighbors who borrow sugar and milk occasionally? Has your kitchen become a fast-food franchise? Has your living room stood vacant and unused as a display area for your best furniture? I want you to know that your home, whether appraised at $20,000 or $120,000, can be a hub of Christian service.

Your kitchen table and your inexpensive dishes can be valuable tools in a needed and effective ministry—the ministry of friendship and outreach to the Christian and non-Christian alike.

Years ago everything centered around the home. There were potlucks, picnics in the back yard, and eight extra people for Sunday dinner. The coffee was always perking; there were homemade cookies in the jar for anyone that might stop by; and the piano bench was frequently pushed up to the end of the table to squeeze in one more new friend.

But we've become too busy with other things, too hung up on having the right kind of china and the perfect menu. And we've also become unwilling to put forth the extra effort.

A few years ago, my husband and I moved to a new city. We didn't know anyone. Our marriage was not in good shape, and we were living through an extremely tough financial crisis. I don't mind telling you that we needed friends.

We joined a church and became quite involved. Before long we had met a number of people who spoke to us in the hall on Sunday morning or chit-chatted at choir practice on Wednesday night.

I realize they didn't know we were living through a great many struggles. I know they couldn't tell by looking at us that peanut butter and bread were the only things on our shelf from time to time. But we would have given anything to have heard one person say, "Hey, I don't know what I can throw together, but come on over and we'll raid the refrigerator." But no one did.

Finally, we began inviting folks to our house for dinner or after church on Sunday nights. We thought maybe things would be different if we made the first effort. We found, however, that people were always glad to come to our house; but that was usually as far as it went.

As the holidays approached, I remember how lonely we were. We went through the entire holiday season without so much as an invitation to share a Christmas cookie or a cup of cranberry juice. Yes, I cried. I wondered if there were something wrong with us. No one seemed to care or want our friendship.

Believe me, we wouldn't have cared if their house were drafty and we had to sit on the floor. It wouldn't have mattered what they served or what they served it on. A paper plate would have done just fine. We would have been thrilled beyond words just to have been invited—*anywhere.*

We needed friendship, not gourmet cooking. We needed conversation, not fine china. We needed people, not their sterling silver dishes.

I have since found out that most people thought we were probably overrun by friends. After all, I traveled, did a lot of public speaking, sang in various churches . . . why, we probably had friends and social engagements running out our ears. And because everyone thought that, no one did anything.

There are many people just like us. They are sitting in the pews of your church, singing in your choir, and they are lonely. They need your friendship, your home, and your time. And they need it now, not three months from now when you get your new living room couch, not after Christmas when you complete your matching set of crystal goblets, not a year from now when you quit working and have more time to fix fancy four-layer tortes.

If you've been praying for the Lord to show you something you can do that could be your personal ministry, pray about this: Which two or three new couples a month should we ask into our home? Have them together or separately. Serve dinner or just dessert and coffee. But get to know them. Make them feel welcome in your home. Let them know you're interested in them.

You will find that some are new Christians and need fellowship desperately. You may find that some don't know what it is to trust Jesus Christ as Savior. You will probably discover that some are going through deep water and need a helping hand. And

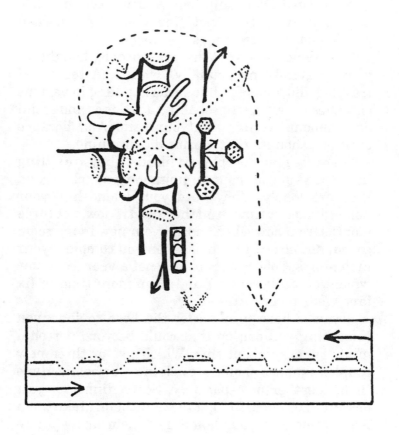

Are you sure you want me to find your house?

some will be mature Christian people who will minister to you and give you the lift and companionship you need.

This ministry is so needed in our churches today. We all know how transient Americans have become. More than ever before, there are people attending and joining our churches who are strangers in our cities.

And when the holiday seasons come and we get so busy with the same family and friends we see year after year, who thinks about those people separated from their loved ones, perhaps financially unable to do anything about it? Remember, we *meet* people in church and Sunday school, but friendships are cultivated in our living rooms.

I have a friend who used to live in our city. She and her husband had a nice home, but she wasn't the world's best housekeeper. When we would arrive at the front door, many times we weren't sure she was expecting us. She would have to move one project or the other out of the way so we could sit down. She never looked quite put together. But we were always met with the words and affection that made us feel we were really welcome.

We were invited for dinner many times, but the times I enjoyed most were when we just dropped in. We would have to move a stack of dishes to find the cookies she "knew she had somewhere." We would laugh and catch up on the news and talk about the kids and the plants and the new fence.

But the thing that was best about that home and those people was I knew I could come dressed up or dressed down. I knew I was welcome whether my mood was good or bad. And I knew I could have knocked on their door any time of the day or night, and I would have been welcome. I wasn't the only one who felt that way, because they shared their home and gave of themselves to others. I'm so incredibly thankful for that.

My husband and I have always enjoyed entertaining. I must admit I'm more excited about cooking for twenty people than I am about cleaning up later. But I still think it's worth it (well, almost always).

There was the time just a couple of months ago that my husband announced to me that he had invited eight people for dinner that night—without checking with me first. After a brief intermission for fuming, I quickly started to plan the menu and my shopping list. When I had returned from the store and was elbow deep in three pounds of hamburger, it suddenly dawned on me that I was scheduled to speak that night, about twenty-five miles away.

As I stood there with ground beef pressed under my fingernails, onions sautéing in butter, and panic brewing in my mind, I came very close to making my husband, who so skillfully got us into the mess, call the people and give them an honest rain check.

Instead, I looked at the clock, did a little calculating, and set everyone in motion. The leaves literally leaped into the middle of the dining room table. The casserole cooperated in throwing itself together. The cake was iced at the lukewarm stage, and the salad was tossed so fast it didn't even realize the green pepper was missing.

I threw on some different clothes, gave my husband instructions as to when to turn on the oven, perk the coffee, and put the ice in the glasses, and told him, "Occupy till I return!"

I made it to the meeting on schedule and didn't even have time to worry about how I looked. I spoke and sang; and at the close I announced there were eight people sitting in my living room by now, and I couldn't linger too long to talk.

As I drove back to the house and up the driveway, I was not totally convinced it was all worth it. I knew that if Larry did this again in the near future, he might not live to regret it.

I walked in the back door, glanced happily at the oven (which was on and at the right temperature), and strolled casually to the living room to greet our guests—all of whom had never been to our home before and were probably wondering what kind of ding-a-lings we were.

Considering the circumstances, the evening had all the makings of a disaster. But it wasn't. When everyone had gone home, we agreed it was one of the nicest evenings we had spent in a long time. The people were terrific, and we were glad we had gotten to know them. I think I would do it all again, just to meet them.

What a ministry we can have without ever leaving our homes, if we're willing to share what we have. You don't have to buy anything new. Just be willing to share what God has already given you.

Volunteer your home for a Bible study; have the youth group over for popcorn and soft drinks; invite each new couple that joins your Sunday school class.

The other day I bought a streusel cake mix for $1.62. I could make that, fix grapefruit halves topped with a maraschino cherry, make a pot of coffee, and have five gals in for coffee some morning this week—all for about $5.50.

My placemats, coffee mugs, and the white dishes I bought on sale at an import store would work just fine. Decorative napkins and the centerpiece I have on my kitchen table anyway would furnish the added touch. For the investment of thirty minutes of my time, I could have a positive effect on the lives of five other people. If out of those five, two were neighbors I had never met, who had never been in a Christian home or had never had one-to-one contact with a child of God—think what an investment my $5.50 would be!

Why, that could be the beginning of a friendship that could result in that neighbor coming to know Jesus Christ—*definitely* worth my time and effort.

And while I'm on the subject . . . how long has it been since your family entertained non-Christians in your home?

It amazes me as I travel how often I see people busy doing nothing but edifying the saints. They flit from one Bible study to another. They attend Christian luncheons and church dinners. They belong to three Christian organizations and serve on umpteen evangelical committees. I want to know when they have time to do something practical with what they're learning!

I'm all for fellowship and Bible study, but if what we are storing away can't be relevantly communicated to people who need the gospel, then what is the purpose?

We can apply a lot of what we learn to our marriages, our homes, and our churches, but what about applying it to some basic witnessing? There are many people who, except for a passing hello, go for weeks without talking to anyone except those in their local Christian world.

We need to get out and meet people—people we can't communicate with through evangelical phrases only, people who need to hear the practicality of being a Christian in terms they understand. To hide in the safety and comfort of our Christian circles is to limit the work of the Holy Spirit. I, for one, am going to do something with those verses I've learned—besides writing them on 3 by 5 cards.

Take your knowledge, your trust in the Lord, your spiritual courage and strength, and your Christian home, and ask God for a ministry.

As part of my work I was interviewing a man in Singapore one day. He seemed to be very nervous and hesitant. Finally he looked at me and said very slowly, in broken English, "I am embarrassed because my ministry is very small. I do not preach at large meetings, and I have never been part of any mass rallies. I'm afraid I have nothing exciting to tell you about my work, for it is very simple. However, the Lord has given me the privilege of winning thirty-one Hindus to the Lord—one by one—in my home."

I sat there and cried.

Our idea of effective ministries gets way out of whack sometimes. No ministry outweighs another if we're all doing what God wants us to do. Winning people to Christ one by one in your home can be one of the most dynamic ministries going on anywhere in the world today.

Don't underestimate what you and your pots and pans can accomplish for God. Open up your home.

Make the lonely and the lost welcome. And keep the coffee hot—because if I'm ever in your neighborhood, I'd love to stop by.

Don't assume that those who write or sing or pastor a church wouldn't want to come to your home. They need friends, too!

By the way, have you had your preacher and his wife over for popcorn lately?

Chapter 5

How Does One Behave Around an Evangelical?

If someone were to walk up to me on the street and ask me, "How does one behave around an evangelical?" my immediate answer would probably be: *"Very carefully."*

The evangelical Christian world in which I have lived all my life is still hard for me to understand at times. Other times it is just plain funny.

A friend pointed at one future speaking engagement on my calendar not long ago and said, "When you go here, make sure you don't refer to 'God' or the 'Lord.' Use the name 'Jesus.' They like that."

Last week, a friend who belongs to the same denomination that was holding the convention I was to speak at, said: "Just insert the word 'sanctification' three times while you are speaking. They'll love you."

These things were said in humor, and I laughed in response; but what they implied was true. Allow me to speak bluntly, perhaps even to preach a bit.

Evangelical society is, indeed, a complicated world all its own. It has its lines of demarcation, its geographical variances, its doctrinal differences. Its people agree, for the most part, on what a Christian is. But they all hold vastly different personal opinions concerning how one should act.

If I were going to give an orientation course to a new Christian before leading him into the evangelical community, I guess these are the things I would feel he needs to know in order to survive in good standing—things I cannot tell him, but with tongue in cheek, wish I could:

(1) Buy a covered dish! Now I can't overestimate the importance of this. Make sure it's a size that can hold a salad, a vegetable, or a meat casserole. Your entire social life might depend on this one purchase. Keep it clean and ready for use at all times. And whatever you do, don't make the mistake of ever using it for your good chicken recipe with the terrific wine sauce—that "wonderful flavor" could ruin your whole future!

(2) Don't spend too much time with unsaved people. No one will ever assume that you are having a positive effect; they will think you are flirting with the world. You'll be a lot safer from criticism if you insulate yourself totally by socializing with other Christians. I've never exactly understood how you do this *and* reach the people who need to know Jesus Christ at the same time. But if what the believers think of you is more important than being a friend to the lost, don't venture out too far.

(3) Offer to keep the records in your Sunday school class. It will help you to get to know people more quickly. You will be able to pick up valuable information—like who brings their

Bible to church, who gives an offering, who is punctual, and who is faithful. You will find these facts helpful when you begin learning how to grade people spiritually.

(4) Work hard on your evangelical vocabulary. You will find that your use of key phrases and verbal responses will affect your position in the spiritual placement exam. It also reveals your denomination (which we all know is a matter of life and death). You will find that in most evangelical circles the unspoken rule of thumb is: "As soon as you begin to sound and act like us, you are one of us."

Now I know a lot of this sounds facetious, but sadly, most of it is true.

Many times I have listened to the bright, unaffected testimony of new Christians, only to hear them interrupt themselves to apologize for not using the "right terms" to explain what God has done for them.

I always want to ask, "What *right terms*?" I don't even understand some of the expressions used, so I'm sure the whole evangelical world is rather overwhelming to a new Christian. After all, they are entering a community that bases its beliefs on the Word of God, that promotes the concept of abundant life, that talks about the freedom from sin found in Jesus Christ.

With the marvelous glow of a newborn babe in Christ, they often find themselves unprepared for what they really find. The evangelical can be plastic, unforgiving, judgmental, and fresh out of stock on the fruit of the Spirit.

I myself am occasionally uncomfortable in the

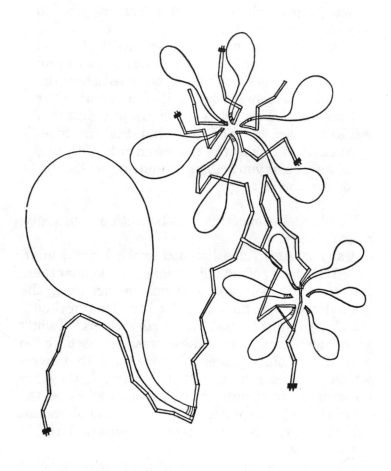

I want to be plugged in!

evangelical world, and I grew up in it! At times I am forced to walk tiptoe through legalism and narrow-mindedness and attitudes that are, I'm sure, far removed from what God intended. For a long time I behaved very guardedly around other Christians, because even though many said they loved me, I knew that was only the opening line to a speech that informed me they didn't.

Christians can be cruel, politically motivated, and petty to the point of absurdity.

I have watched the people of the church give a new member the right hand of fellowship and never talk to him again. I have seen the manipulation of power and of people—all under the umbrella of "the direction of God."

And I'm sorry to say that I have witnessed, on many occasions, the complete bulldozing of a person's life, job, and future by people who would never think of missing Wednesday night prayer meeting.

So many Christians forget that being more Christ-like should be our goal; the priorities of our lives begin to center on our strategy to be accepted and patted on the back by the people who can get us on the right committee next year.

If I were asked what I feel is the most devastating weakness of the evangelical world, my answer would be *gossip*—the gossip of both men and women alike. And the thing that is most dangerous about our brand of gossip is that we try to justify it by making it sound holy and anointed of the Lord.

Somehow we feel that we Christians have a special ability to handle privileged information, as well as a spiritual duty to bring it out in the open. "Now I really wouldn't tell anyone else all these things about

John and Sue's marriage, but I thought you could pray more intelligently if you had all the details."

"I know that Stephen is a good friend of yours and think you ought to know what I found out so that you will be able to give him some spiritual guidance when he comes to you."

"Did you know that Jean hasn't been in Sunday school for three weeks? Maybe there is trouble with the marriage. Perhaps if you call her, the Lord will direct you to say just the right thing so that we'll be able to find out the problem."

The sad thing is that maybe the problem was that Jean didn't feel welcome in the Sunday school class.

Prayer meetings—especially small ones—can also be a catchall for gossip. Often we spend more time giving long, detailed prayer requests than we do praying.

Backbiting and gossip are still the two most effective ways of turning off a new Christian, injuring a seasoned one, and tearing down the foundation of a local church.

So also the tongue is a small thing, but what enormous damage it can do. A great forest can be set on fire by one tiny spark. And the tongue is a flame of fire. It is full of wickedness and poisons every part of the body. And the tongue is set on fire by hell itself, and can turn our whole lives into a blazing flame of destruction and disaster (James 3:5,6, TLB).

How do you behave around an evangelical? Again I say—"Very carefully."

When God's Word calls Christians "a special

people," I don't think He meant this should be the case because of our legalistic mentality, our attention to pettiness, and our self-proclaimed position as judge of the world.

Rather, I feel He meant us to be different because of our strong convictions about our important beliefs, our great assets as children of God, and our good examples in this world. If we are not unique in a better way, then why be unique at all? It surely makes God look bad.

I would be totally unfair if I left you with the impression that every Christian is legalistic and judgmental, and every part of the evangelical world is more interested in gossip than God. For, of course, that isn't true. I have chosen to live and function and thrive in the evangelical world. I am active in and committed to my own church. I have great Christian friends, and I am privileged to know some genuinely Christlike people who have influenced my life positively and have given me help and direction that I believe came from God.

I just feel we have to be honest and aware of the pitfalls that all of us, if we are not careful, can fall into. I, too, have problems with prejudice and my own set of standards that I am guilty of forcing on other people. I, too, judge others when I shouldn't and have passed on information that was none of my business.

I have tried to patch up things that only God can patch up. I have put aside what I have known God wanted me to do in order to feel I was accepted. I have compromised, and I have sinned miserably.

I also know that God is not pleased with those qualities in His children.

And whatever you do, do it heartily, as to the Lord and not to men, knowing that from the Lord you will receive the reward of the inheritance; for you serve the Lord Christ (Col. 3:23,24).

Sometimes it seems it is just as difficult to be the kind of person God wants us to be in the evangelical community as it is in the world.

It is easy to substitute the business of Christian life and the myriad of meetings for the consistent work that needs to be done between us and God. It is easy to forget that fellowship with the believers doesn't take the place of one-to-one fellowship with the One in charge of our lives.

We can sit right in the center of the inner circle of the evangelical world and be far from God. We can be in seminary and be cold to the moving of the Holy Spirit. Some of that is due to the quirks of the Christian world, but most of it is a result of our weak relationship with Jesus Christ.

We can always find reasons to criticize and complain when we put our trust in the ruling boards of our churches. We can always turn cynical if we are more involved in politics than in the winning of the lost.

The people who make up the strong and effective church of God are those who know that the rock of their faith is Christ Jesus. They are those who are involved first in keeping their hearts right with God. They are those whose faith and beliefs are unshakable. They are the ones who exemplify the fruit of the Spirit.

These masses of the redeemed who understand what it is to be a Christian are the church triumphant, the church victorious, the church alive and well. This part of the church does not hand out stamps of approval or pass down judgments. It simply invites you to join in the praising of God, the loving encouragement of the believers, and the spreading of the gospel to those who need the changing power of Jesus Christ in their lives.

The Church's one foundation
Is Jesus Christ her Lord;
She is His new creation
By water and the word:
From heaven He came and sought her
To be His holy bride;
With His own blood He bought her,
And for her life He died.

Elect from every nation,
Yet one o'er all the earth,
Her charter of salvation,
One Lord, one faith, one birth;
One holy Name she blesses,
Partakes one holy food,
And to one hope she presses,
With every grace endued.*

*Samuel J. Stone, "The Church's One Foundation."

Chapter 6

Now That I Have Children, What Am I To Do With Them?

The water was dripping off my umbrella and splattering onto the plastic garbage bag spread across my knees. My tennis shoes were wet; my jeans and old shirt were covered by an ancient, no longer water-repellent raincoat. My hair spray had turned to glue, and my eyelashes were sticking together. But believe it or not, I was having a good time.

I looked around—no one looked any better than I did—and I thought to myself, "You've come a long way, Baby. Who ever would have thought you would be sitting in the rain watching your son play soccer and liking it?" My thoughts were interrupted as I saw the ball roll into dangerous territory, and without thinking I actually yelled, "Kick it, Jason! Get in there and kick it. Come on, Timbers!"

How my kids have changed my life! They have turned this precise, overorganized, unbending, over-dressed lady into an almost regular person.

Sometimes I watch my kids walking toward me, across a parking lot, a sports field, or the school lawn, and I want to say to someone, "I'm their mother, you know." It is incredible that I, who never cooked a meal until I was twenty-six; I, who never dreamed about white picket fences or baking chocolate-chip cookies; I, who never saw any joy in kids eating with their fingers or getting into my makeup—I actually want to say, "I'm their mother." I've managed to live through eleven years of it. And there are even moments here and there that I can look back upon and feel I've done some things right.

Melissa was born on Christmas Day, 1968. She is like me in a lot of ways. I find her easy to cry with, to laugh with, and (I'm afraid) to fight with.

She is also my demonstrative child. She has no trouble throwing her arms around people and making them feel warm and welcome. She opens each birthday present with storybook delight, and gives you every detail of every story, whether you want to hear it or not. How I love her!

Jason was born in October, 1970. He is adopted. I will never forget the day we got him. I had to fly to another state to pick him up. Larry couldn't go because we hadn't had much notice, so I boarded a plane alone at six-thirty in the morning with an empty infant seat and a diaper bag. I weighed some three hundred pounds at the time and was dressed in a long, flowing caftan and dangling earrings. To say the least, I got a lot of attention.

Upon arriving, I was eager to get out. Pushing my way into the aisle long before the door was open, my fellow travelers had all the time they needed to stare at me and become all the more curious about what I was carrying.

Finally, no longer able to resist the temptation, I looked around and in a loud voice announced that just

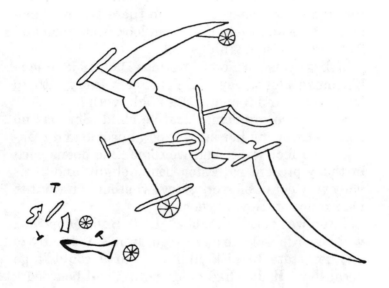

Helping my son with his model did not benefit our relationship.

before I left home I had watched Oral Roberts, and he had said: "Today, something good is going to happen to you!" . . . and I thought I should be prepared.

Well, something terrific did happen to us. We added a tiny, bald, wrinkled human being to our family. I will never forget that day, because at no other time have I been more overwhelmed by the responsibility of parenthood.

The nurse gave me some formula to take on the plane, the mother's little packet of information and samples of baby cereal, and had me sign the papers. When the preliminaries were over, she went around the corner and returned with a wiggly bundle, wrapped in pink-and-blue striped flannel. Nonchalantly, she handed me a human life and said, "Here you go."

In just thirty seconds, my every fault rushed through my mind. I wanted to say, "Do you know what you're doing? You're giving a real live person to someone who isn't qualified!" I wanted to confess that I was inconsistent, easily irritated, not particularly domestic, and that there were probably lots of people better equipped for this job than I was. I looked down at that tiny person and felt overwhelmed with responsibility and inadequacy.

I had been a mother for almost two years, but never before had I really felt the awesomeness of it as at that moment. But I reached out and took him, and loved him, and kept him. I figured he'd just have to put up with me.

I got on another plane a few hours later to take him home. This time the infant seat was full, and the diaper bag seemed logical.

However, I did manage to have some fun on this

flight as well. Anyone who looked very closely could tell he was very newly born. When they couldn't stand it any longer and asked how old he was, I must admit that I delighted in looking up and saying, "Forty-eight hours," with no further explanation. On the trip down I had appeared to be a ding-a-ling, but on the way back I made up for it by coming off as a very strong woman!

I soon adjusted to having two small children—I set my alarm for an earlier hour on Sunday mornings and learned how to get twice as much done in the same amount of time.

The era of booties, bottles, and burps seemed to go pretty well. I learned to count to ten, do the vacuuming during naps, and keep the children dressed to perfection most of the time. They both walked early, talked well, showed signs of superior intelligence, and responded to yes and no.

But one day I woke up to realize that the booties had grown into tennis shoes, the play telephone had been replaced with the real thing, and those cute little stretch suits and plastic tricycles were now jeans, T-shirts, and dirt bikes.

My questions were no longer hard ones like, "Shall I choose strained peas or mashed bananas for lunch?" but, "How do I instill self-esteem? How do I communicate the importance of choosing the right friends? How do I help these precious children cultivate values and priorities and the sort of stability that will affect them positively the rest of their lives?"

My first impulse was to run away or to put an ad in the paper to see if anybody wanted to take it from there. I would even have offered to throw in their clothes, their clutter, and their trundle beds. After all, if I wasn't even impressed with my maturity, my judgment, my self-esteem, how in the world was I going to help shape their lives?

I didn't really know . . . but I did know I loved them, and I knew without a shadow of a doubt that God had given us those two lives—and the greatest challenge we had ever faced. I just had to hang in there, and I still am.

There have been nights I've crawled into bed totally destroyed by a day that seemed to indicate I hadn't done one thing right. Many times I've turned over and wept, saying to God, "I should never have become a mother. I'm not the type and never will be. I've got these two kids. I love them deeply, but what am I to do with them? I'm obviously doing everything wrong.

"If they can't even remember to brush their teeth, Lord, how are they going to remember that they have all the potential in the world? If they don't see a need for soap and water, how will they realize the need for biblical principles in everyday life?"

And through the tears, I have heard that Friend "who sticketh closer than a brother" say, "I'll help you. You're not a failure. You've done a lot of things right, too; and remember, I'm in this thing with you."

And when I stop to really think about it, I know He's right. We would be proud to take our kids anywhere. They like people. They can carry on a good conversation. They don't embarrass us. They're doing well in school. They love us and tell us so. They are aware of many of their own problems and, for the most part, are willing to discuss them. You're right, Lord. We haven't done such a bad job.

Being a mother has not come easily for me. I am not

by nature domestic or artsy or stay-at-homish. Many stereotyped characteristics of motherhood totally escape me. But with my dependence on God, a sound mind, and a deep love for my children, we are making it in good shape.

So here we are. A new day. My kids are in the fourth and fifth grades. They are studying things I've never heard of and doing math I don't understand. They are growing by metric centimeters and letting me know by various ways and means that my most difficult years are yet ahead of me.

Well, I can't run away anymore. I've accumulated too much stuff. And I can't give the kids away. No one would ever be able to understand what I've done with them so far. And besides, I've matured a lot. I like being their mother, for better or for worse—and more often, for richer or for poorer. I'm afraid they are stuck with me now.

However, it's beyond me how parents face their responsibility of raising kids in this day and age without God's help. Even as a Christian parent I am sometimes scared and frequently very lonely. Even though I am rather contemporary in a lot of things, I am old fashioned and conservatively opinionated about many others. And I wonder sometimes if I'm standing all by myself on certain issues.

I am accused, just as you are, of being a mean parent on certain issues. I am informed, during moments of encouragement, that I'm the only mother in the world who thinks as I do. I have been told I have strange taste in clothes, fix funny meals, and seldom feel like doing anything fun. Now, that isn't true, of course, but I will admit my sense of timing seems to be consistently off.

The day I make an effort to meet the kids at the back door with a smile and hot, homemade cookies is the day they both come in mad because they've argued all the way home. The night I decide to do something fun and set my work aside is the same night all the kids are meeting at Phillip's to build a spook house. (Next to that, playing with mother sounds dull.) The morning I arise and greet the kids with a cheery good morning as they come through the kitchen door is always the morning no one wants to talk.

Just as I'm not alone in experiencing these little setbacks in motherhood, I'm sure I'm not alone in the big issues, either. It's just that I can't always see or hear the parents who are on my team. It's about time we make a little noise and encourage each other!

I have begun to think I am part of a dying society . . . a fading group of soldiers marching the opposite direction from the rest of the army. I believe with all my heart that parents should be in charge of their children. I believe children should learn to dress up on Sunday morning and sit still in church. I also feel they should be encouraged to listen, and not be handed a pencil and doodle pad as soon as the sermon begins.

It's my opinion that children should know how to sit down and eat correctly, not just stand at a counter and shovel it in. I think families should eat in the dining room occasionally, with the candles lit and soft music playing in the background.

Further, I am of the opinion that children should have their own domestic responsibilities, not because it is a way of earning an allowance, but because they are part of a family that pitches in to create a home and an atmosphere they can enjoy and be proud of. Children should know that their parents are going to check their homework, listen to their oral book reports, and examine their grade cards.

I believe in obedience—with understanding—and discipline with explanations. I am one hundred percent for rules and regulations. I am a pusher for love, shown through hugs and kisses and special gifts and birthday parties and long walks and intimate talks. However, I also believe in love shown through demanding something of your children: conduct that will prepare them for any situation; obedience that teaches them about all the things in life that must be done whether one wants to or not; and some hard work, the exercise that affects everything they choose to do well or halfway.

Most of all, I believe in respect. And, wow, do I feel lonely on this issue! I listen to the way children speak to their parents at the grocery store and gasp when I realize the parents don't even raise an eyebrow. I hear the stories of how children treat their school teachers, their choir directors, their Sunday school teachers—and for the most part, they get away with it.

I must confess that we are going through a lippy, "Who do you think you are?" stage in our house. My kids, just like yours, try to see how much they can get away with. They pick up the attitudes of the kids they are around in school all day and think some of it is cute. Evidently, the only difference between our house and many others is that here we don't think it's funny; nor do we ignore it when our children are disrespectful.

Three-year-old children have ordered me out of

chairs so they could sit down. I have heard five-year-olds tell their parents they are stupid, and the parents have turned around and bought them twenty-dollar toys to try to change their opinions.

Whatever happened to the tradition of addressing older people by their last names? Whatever happened to "please" and "thank you"? In fact, whatever happened to manners in general?

Where are the children who've been taught to respect other people's property or to eat what's put in front of them? Where are the children who don't interrupt a conversation? And where are the children who appreciate the things people do for them?

They're becoming very hard to find because we have forgotten the word "respect."

I'm all for reading books, for parents' sharing groups, and for helpful hints from the family pediatrician. But I do not believe God ever intended us to feed a child the nonsense that he should always have the freedom to express himself and do what he wants to do.

Even Dr. Spock is questioning his own ideology. Two articles recently reported his surprise that babies brought up by his ideas on discipline have turned out to be disrespectful young adults.

Pile the books in the corner for a few days and take a good look at your kids. Listen to how they talk to you. Now, for goodness sake, start using some God-given common sense. Remind yourself who's in charge. Read God's Word. See what He has to say about what's right and what's wrong.

We love to quote that verse: "Train up a child in the way he should go: and when he is old, he will not depart from it" (Prov. 22:6). The word is *train*—not "let it happen." The word is *train*—not "suggest." Training is hard work. *We don't train anymore.* We car pool and sign our kids up for twelve different activities instead. Consequently, we have kids who play an instrument, kick a good ball, know how to use a calculator—and tell their folks where to get off.

I will never forget a statement a child psychologist made one day while speaking to a group of mothers. She said, "How can you expect your kids to respect God, whom they cannot see, when they don't respect you? How can you expect them to be obedient to God's Word when *you* have never taught them obedience or expected it from them?" These words have stuck with me. As a Christian parent, I want my children to know who is head of our house: God is first and, whether they like it or not, parents are next in line.

There are days when I feel as if I'm fighting a losing battle. There are times when I want to throw my hands up and quit. There are days I feel all alone against our permissive society. *But they are my kids.* I'm responsible for them. And I plan to stick to my guns.

I pray there are many others who feel as I do. We need each other's support and encouragement. But if you aren't with me, that's okay, because the Lord is with me, and He keeps on saying: "I am with you—you're doing a good job. And remember—you may be the mother, but I am God. I will never leave you nor forsake you."

I am so grateful for that, because the kids just came through the door. One doesn't understand her homework, and the other one had a fight with the kid across the street. And I'm faced with training again.

Chapter 7

The Tragedy of the
Might Have Been

I was seventeen years old, had just graduated from high school, and was waiting tables, as well as working on the music staff, at "Camp of the Woods" in New York's Adirondack Mountains.

It was Sunday morning, and this was my day to accompany the soloist and play for the congregational singing at the services. Frank Boggs had been the guest musician for the week, and I knew he was to sing that morning. But as I walked into the tabernacle, I had not seen the music or been informed of his selections. That didn't particularly bother me, though, since I felt I could hold my own. Besides, I figured he wouldn't throw anything too difficult at me on such short notice.

Just a few minutes after I sat down at the keyboard to warm up, people started gathering. Mr. Boggs strolled in, said good morning, and pulled his music from his briefcase. I had always loved his singing, and I was rather excited about the privilege of playing for him. But my excitement turned to terror as he opened the sheet music and placed it on the rack in front of me. Assuming he would be assigned a competent accompanist, he had chosen to sing, "I Walked Today Where Jesus Walked"—in five sharps!

I wanted to die—or at least hide under the piano bench. My body went cold, my fingers stiffened, and more than anything I wanted to tell him I couldn't handle it. But I didn't. He turned to me and said that since people were already coming in and since he was sure I was familiar with that piece, we would just do it cold and not run through it beforehand.

Well, we did it cold all right—very cold—and very poorly, I might add. That he even sang it all the way through was due only to his professional ability. He certainly didn't get any help from me. I don't know for sure what key I played it in.

When it was over, I felt as if my life was over. I didn't ever want to look anyone in the face again, particularly Frank Boggs, who I'm sure had never been through such a long and grueling four minutes in all his life.

For the rest of the day, all I could think was: "I wish I hadn't always avoided playing sharps. If only I had listened and worked harder. I wish I weren't so dumb." I also added that I would never play the piano again.

But like most of you who have had similar experiences, I didn't die of humiliation, and within twenty-four hours I *did* play the piano again. What I didn't realize was that for one day I had had a close brush with a deadly disease called the "If-I-had, if-I-hadn't" syndrome.

The advanced stages of this disease are not prevalent among young people. Severe cases are usually found in adults over thirty years old. The two main causes are blame and excuse, two deep infections that cause deterioration in many areas of life.

The damaging effects of the disease are usually manifested in unrecognized potential, lack of motivation, and the dulling acceptance of not being what you know you could be.

You could have the disease, for it is rampant and tends to attack just about everyone in various degrees. Some have found a cure, some get temporary relief, and some have learned to live every day with the nagging symptoms. These symptoms are easily recognized; they appear first as negative thoughts, and then as defensive statements, such as:

"If only I had finished college—gotten my degree—I would be doing something worthwhile today."

"If I had spent more time with my children when they were younger, I wouldn't be having problems with them now."

"If I had taken better care of my teeth years ago, I wouldn't have these dental bills."

"If I had known what I know now, I would have handled my marriage differently. Then I wouldn't be in this mess."

"If I had had different parents, I wouldn't have all the hangups I have."

"If I were as talented as you, I would be able to really accomplish something."

I could write pages of illustrations, but I think you get the point.

Are you one of those people who justify what you are or are not today because of what you wish you had or hadn't done? Do you catch yourself blaming your inadequacies on what has happened to you and the way you've been treated?

Then let me warn you. This disease not only can be crippling; if untreated, it can be terminal. There is a

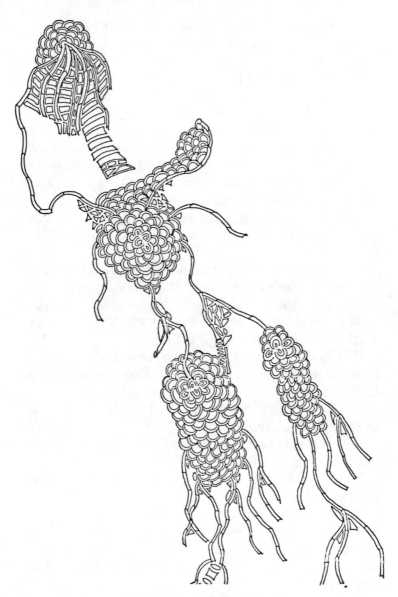

I wish I hadn't done that!

point at which the deteriorating infection of the wish-I-had, wish-I-hadn't syndrome becomes the tragedy of the "might have been."

A man I have known for a long time is in his mid-fifties. He's very gifted, very bright. He has all the ingredients of a dynamic personality, all the abilities of an achiever, all the knowledge of an expert in his field.

But he is paralyzed. Oh, you'd never know it to look at him, for he appears to be in good health. Those of us who know him well, however, know he is paralyzed by his past.

After all these years, part of him has died ... smothered by all the bitterness, hurt, unforgiveness, and deep anger over what people did to him forty years ago. He is being strangled by the inability to forget his mistakes and what someone said to him a quarter of a century ago.

This man has lived all his life in evangelical circles; he has worked in Christian organizations, and has sat through more gospel messages than most of you, I'm sure. But he is dying. He is hard and cynical and totally untrusting. He flits from one job to the other, one church pew to the other, always ending up angry and blaming everybody else for what does or doesn't happen in his life.

The fact is he hates himself for who he is, for where he came from, for what he hasn't been able to handle, and for the many times he has walked out and quit.

He is still griping about the same things he griped about twenty years ago. When he shows his feelings and his mistrust, you realize he's in exactly the same spot he's been in since you met him years ago.

And I always leave him with the awesome feeling

that what he has is terminal. As I walk away, I say to myself, "Just think what he could have been."

I wonder if God doesn't say the same thing.

I never want to be at the place where people make that remark when they walk away from me. Lord, help me never to let that happen.

Not long ago, my daughter asked me a question about my past. It came as a result of a discussion of love and marriage and moral conduct. The question she asked was very personal, and I will never forget how I felt as she looked up at me and waited for an answer.

In thirty seconds of time, a myriad of thoughts went through my mind.

"I wish I hadn't made so many mistakes."

"I wish I had the right words."

"I wish I could avoid being honest."

"I wish she had a mother she could be proud of."

And then I realized I'm not what I used to be; I am who I am. I explained to her that I had made some mistakes, and I hoped what I had learned from them would be valuable not only to me, but to her too. I pointed out that there was a time in my life when I didn't depend on God to help me make the right choices, and therefore I had taken a lot of wrong turns.

I told her that God loved me and was patient, and that finally I had realized that I needed Him in my life. And when I asked His forgiveness and let Him take control of my life, He gave me a new life—one He is using and developing every day. I finished by saying, "I'm sorry for a lot of things I've done, but I can't waste my life feeling I'm no good just because of my past. I have a new life to live, and I want you to know that living for Jesus is the best choice you can make."

If I were to think hard, I could think of enough "If-I-hads" and "if-I-hadn'ts" to keep me from doing anything. The greatest escape artists in the world are those who hide behind their pasts. And Christians frequently become very good at it.

Remember that the Lord never said to one of us, "Because of all the stupid mistakes and bad choices you've made, there is a limit to what I can do with you."

Instead, He says: "If anyone is in Christ, he is a new creation; old things have passed away; behold, all things have become new" (2 Cor. 5:17).

I'm sure there isn't one of us who wishes he hadn't done something different in his life. But God doesn't expect us to go back and relive our lives. He doesn't ask us to take a crash course on all the subjects we didn't excel in when we had the chance. He offers forgiveness for the mistakes we've made, gives us a clean slate to replace the smudged one, and asks for our willingness to give Him the rest of our lives.

Listen to what Paul wrote in Colossians 3:10,11:

You are living a brand new kind of life that is continually learning more and more of what is right, and trying constantly to be more and more like Christ who created this new life within you. In this new life one's nationality or race or education or social position is unimportant; such things mean nothing. Whether a person has Christ is what matters, and He is equally available to all (TLB).

73

The day we accept Him as Savior, we are no longer just the product of what has happened to us so far; we are the embryo of a new life, with a new future and all the assets that a child of God receives.

Now, get on with it so that next year you won't be saying, "I wish I had taken the advice I read in that book."

If you've blown it with your kids, don't sit around in turmoil thinking about what you could have done. Ask God what you should do from this moment on, and ask Him for the wisdom and consistency to do it.

If your parents never showed you affection and now you can't wrap your arms around your loved ones, quit blaming your mom and dad. Ask the Lord to teach you how to hug your family and say, "I love you."

If you turned down teaching a Sunday school class because you were thinking, "If only I had studied the Bible as I should have," call back and take the job. There is no better way to learn God's Word and how to apply it than having to prepare a relevant lesson each week.

If you've become irritatingly accepting of being less than you should be, ask God *today* to help you get over the habit of letting your past smother your future. After all, that future could be exciting! You might be pleasantly surprised at what God will do with you.

Brethren, I do not count myself to have apprehended; but one thing I do, forgetting those things which are behind and reaching forward to those things which are ahead, I press toward the goal for the prize of the upward call of God in Christ Jesus (Phil. 3:13,14).

Chapter 8

Christians and The Fine Arts

A few years back, on a leisurely evening at home, Larry and I were watching a symphony concert on the public television station. Appearing with the orchestra were two professional opera stars, a baritone whom I rated as average, and a lyric soprano who was fast driving me up the wall. I was about to plug my ears when Melissa came to the doorway and asked:

"What kind of music is that, Mommy?"

I proceeded to give her a mini-cultural education course, explaining in basic terms what opera was and what those two people did for a living. When I asked if she understood, she put her hands on her hips and exclaimed in disbelief: "You mean that lady gets paid for screaming in that man's ear?"

I fell apart, putting all my culture aside and laughing as I admitted I had been asking myself the same question.

Since that day, Melissa has obviously developed a taste for entertainers who "scream" at each other, and the tables have turned. More than once I have walked into her bedroom, shouted at her to turn her stereo down, and asked above the racket: "You mean people get paid for that?"

The real shocker came the day I asked in a tone of voice that comes only from the speaker system of a mother, "Can't you find something better on that radio to listen to?" She responded, "But Mother— that's Christian music. I found a gospel disco station!"

I turned around, left the room, and closed the door behind me. I knew I had to think about that before I said anything. One part of me was glad she was choosing gospel music; the other part of me didn't want her thinking *that* was Christian music.

I was sitting in a Sunday school class one Sunday morning, and the teacher asked what mental picture we got when we imagined the rapture of the church. It was a very interesting question, and I will never forget one lady's answer. She got a rather ethereal expression on her face and gave this description: "I see the clouds parting—the angels blowing their trumpets and all of us flying through the air to the music of the Mormon Tabernacle Choir, singing 'The Hallelujah Chorus.' "

Well, I don't expect it to be just like that, but the old-fashioned part of me that loves good music doesn't expect us to meet the Lord to the rhythm of a gospel disco group, either.

I am going to take this opportunity to beat my drum and clang my symbols for three matters that are of great importance to me:

(1) The exposure we as Christian parents should be giving our children in the fine arts.

(2) The resurrection of dignified Christian music that prompts the worship of Almighty God, setting forth the gospel of Christ with majesty and warmth.

(3) The role of Christian parents and the church in developing the God-given talents of His children.

Parents complain a lot about their kids' music, the ugly posters on their walls, and their interest in reading something only as deep as a teen movie magazine. In addition to complaining, they can cover their eyes, plug their ears, and try to ignore it, dismissing the whole matter with a hip phrase like, "I guess they're doing their own thing."

Have you ever considered the possibility that they may not be doing their own thing, but rather the only thing they know how to do? What alternatives have you exposed them to?

God says, "Out of the abundance of the heart the mouth speaks. A good man out of the good treasure of his heart brings forth good things; and an evil man out of the evil treasure brings forth evil things" (Matt. 12:33,34).

Your kids soak up a "top-forty" culture during a major part of every day. They walk the halls and eat lunch with twelve- or thirteen-year-olds who are allowed to spend fifteen dollars for a ticket to a rock concert, ride with a sixteen-year-old driver, sit for three hours in the middle of a "hyper" mob, and listen to people who call themselves musicians scream obscenities and tell them it feels good to do it.

When our children are not exposed to anything better, and we are not willing to put forth the effort to see that they also receive an input of quality alternatives, then don't be surprised at the results.

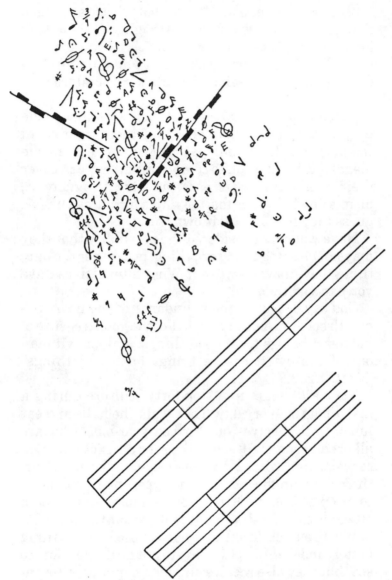

Things don't just always fall into place.

What goes in must come out!

How many opportunities do you afford your children to learn about good music, real art, and the masterpieces of fine literature? Maybe *your* culture is a little stunted, too. Maybe your kids have some right to feel you are naive, a little uninteresting, and unwilling to change your attitudes.

We Christians have a way of misleading ourselves in a safe little world, feeling the Lord will always bless our ignorance of the good things this world has to offer. Too many times we think more highly of the person who prays before he sings than we do of the one who practices before he expects his music to be effective. (I prefer both!)

Many Christians today will live their whole lives without appreciating the hard work of a marvelous painter. They will never hear a Bach fugue or a Debussy impression. They will sit home and watch "Laverne and Shirley" but they will never darken the door of a live theatre for the performance of a dramatic classic.

And their children will be presented with only one alternative to their rock station—the music of your local church. And in some cases, I agree with the kids: it is not much of an alternative.

Now, if you'd like to open your eyes, create some optional input for your kids, and expand your cultural world as well, I have a few suggestions.

Don't start by announcing that you are all going to develop an appreciation for the arts. You'll get voted down, believe me. Start by suggesting some cultural outings that sound like fun. Most symphony orchestras offer a summer concert series in the park. You don't dress up; just take your picnic supper and listen to the music under the atmosphere of the real stars.

In children's concerts sponsored by the symphony, they actually explain the different instruments and the pieces of music presented. And it will help immensely if you find out what music will be performed, do thirty minutes of homework, and explain to the children the significance of what they will hear.

There are art museums, art festivals, and art institutes. Special exhibits of the works of world-famous artists visit different cities during the year.

There are choir concerts, children's theatres, and New York companies that bring outstanding performances of Broadway plays. And there are terrific presentations of Handel's *Messiah* and other classical religious works, as well as superb gospel artists and musicians who come through your area on a regular basis. The weekend issue of your paper will give you many good ideas, as well as make you aware of the free concerts and art fairs available to the public.

Find out what's going on. Open up your world a little. Give your family the chance to soak up something other than what's always thrown at them.

And when you are just around the house, don't forget the classical radio stations and the marvelous fine arts programs now appearing on public television. And it wouldn't hurt to start using those bookshelves with the nick nacks on them to build a good art and music library. Used bookstores make this venture a rare bargain.

We have an antique pump organ in our living room. It works, but my ankles give way when I play it. It's hard to believe that the human voice and an organ like that made up the entire church music program seventy-five years ago.

Now we have orchestras and bell choirs, ensembles, drum sets, guitars, and accompaniment tapes.

I hate to admit, in the midst of all this progress, that I miss enthusiastic congregational singing of hymns like "A Mighty Fortress Is Our God" and "Crown Him with Many Crowns" and the wonderful Sunday night hymn-sings when we sang until we were hoarse.

I'm afraid we might be so intent on creating a new image that we may blur our ability to discern whether we are being edified or entertained. I hope we don't forget that music is a ministry, that it can touch people's hearts. It can encourage and comfort, bring joy and conviction. It is one of the ways we "enter into His gates with thanksgiving and into His courts with praise."

I pray that we don't lose either the music of worship or a certain conscientiousness in using music worthy of the King of Kings. "Make a joyful noise unto the Lord, all the earth: make a loud noise, and rejoice, and sing praise" (Ps. 98:4).

We spend much more time on production numbers than we used to, but look around you when the congregation sings. Hymn number 201 has become simply the next thing in the printed order of worship. People stand, they find the page, but they never really enter in. Very few congregations experience the shaking of the rafters in jubilant praise to the living God.

We are producing many professional gospel musicians, but I feel we've lost the joy of singing. Singing is not only for the trained and extraordinarily talented; it is an expression of every believer's heart. People rarely gather around the piano just to sing anymore. You rarely hear that families sing together in front of the fire or around the Thanksgiving table.

I have been involved in Christian music all my life. No one believes any stronger than I in the development and use of talent, but I don't believe in it to the exclusion of everything else. Christians, in my opinion, are ready for a resurrection of the old hymns of praise, of the times when even the monotone can sing along, of the use of music as an expression of love to God, not just a promotion of the artist.

Why not bring back the old choruses, the great hymns of the church, and even the Sunday night hymn-sings that encourage everybody to sing and enjoy it.

My deepest concern, however, is that if we continue to try so hard to compete with the world, no one will know what Christian music is. Our message is worth a better treatment than it's getting from some sources. When you can't tell if what you're hearing is a gospel song or not, we're in serious trouble. Call me stuffy if you like, but at least you know where to find me on your dial.

When I was a kid, it wasn't very popular for the preacher's daughter to want to become an actress. It wasn't received well by Christian society when teen-aged church members announced they were leaving for college, where they were going to major in radio and television production.

The kid who wanted to be a medical missionary or a school teacher seemed to get an approving pat on the back. The kid who wanted to be a poet or a journalist or an orchestra conductor was put into a category labeled: *Those with whom we ask the Lord to deal.*

Consequently, there are not many Christian White House news writers or born-again symphony conductors. I doubt if there are many believers working in the executive offices of the secular television networks, and Christian involvement in drama is years behind.

Perhaps you have never considered what kind of influence Christians could have in those positions. But I'm happy to say we seem to be finally catching on. For the first time we are discovering that God doesn't make mistakes when He creates us with unique talents and individual personalities.

Parents, you may have a creative child in your house. You may have a future concert violinist, a future television producer, tomorrow's White House news correspondent, or the classical poet of the up-and-coming generation. Make sure you recognize the gifts God has given that child. Don't be guilty of trying to ignore his interests because you would rather he be a missionary doctor or a football player or a business executive.

Before God, you have a responsibility to help your child develop his talent. If he's very young, start by letting him make up a play, and you will be a good audience. Let him tell you, with all the actions, the story he heard in Sunday school; or let him teach you the songs he learned, and you sing along. If he likes to draw, see that he always has paper and colored pencils. Hang up the pictures; let him show them when guests come to visit.

If your child is school age, be aware of his ability to

remember the lyrics and stay on pitch as he sings along with his records. Look closely at his artwork. Read the little essays he writes; if they are good, ask him to write one for you.

Then, *please,* enroll him in piano lessons, art lessons, or a good library program with an introduction to good literature. Expose him to the fine arts.

More than one parent has said to me, "My child is taking piano lessons. She is doing very well, but we don't know how long she'll stick with it. We aren't really that concerned as long as she can sit down and pick out the hymns in the book. Don't you think it's nice for a Christian young person to be able to play gospel hymns?"

My answer to those parents is, "Only if she's learned how to read music, play her scales, and knows good basic theory first."

You know what I think a Christian musician, artist, writer, or actor ought to be? The composite of (a) a tender heart, (b) a creative mind, and (c) the very best training he can get.

I am excited about the fact that many of our churches are beginning to offer marvelous training for young people in the fine arts. They are attracting qualified faculty members and are giving talented Christian young people opportunities to get professional help in the development of their skills and creative dreams.

I am helping to get a similar program off the ground in my own church because I believe in the concept. I believe the church also has a responsibility not only to *develop* talent but to *use* it. Encouraging a talented young person to become the very best in his field may give us a great classical composer with an opportunity to make an impact on the world, not only with his music but with his strong testimony for Jesus Christ.

One day I stood motionless in Rome's Sistine Chapel. Michelangelo's work was breathtaking. I will never know how a few of the tourists managed to walk in and out without ever looking up!

Maybe your child will influence the world some day with a paint brush and a master's touch. Perhaps your child's name will be mentioned along with Chopin, Brahms, and Johann Sebastian Bach. Maybe your child will teach the handicapped to sing or teach the blind a course in fine literature.

As you look at the boy or girl God gave you and wonder about the future, don't forget to look up. God knows. He is the best Consultant you can have on the subject of creative children.

Chapter 9

Things Never Happen Like They Do on TV!

I hate to admit this, but my night cream is not working. Yes, it keeps my skin soft, but unlike the lady who advertises it on television, it doesn't keep my bed from getting messed up, it doesn't keep my hair perfectly coiffured during the night, and it doesn't keep my teeth from feeling grainy. Worst of all, it hasn't taken ten years off my looks.

I finally found a product that cleans the grout between the tiles of my shower stall, but I can't get it to work without putting on grubby clothes and working up a good sweat.

I have been an Ivory girl for so many years that I'm now an Ivory woman. But it's never helped me look terrific in blue jeans or taught me how to ride a horse.

Now for the real heartbreak. Many people have gathered around my dining room table for lunch, dinner, or an occasional piece of pie. But not once has anyone ever picked up one of my dishes, remarked to others about the shine, and exclaimed with delight that they could see themselves in my sparkling plates.

I try so hard, but nothing ever seems to measure up. It wouldn't be so bad if I were the only one affected, but my whole family is obviously out of step, and that really bothers me.

My son came home in deep depression the other day—his Toughskin jeans had died. My daughter just about left home because the shampoo she begged for didn't give her the Farrah Fawcett look.

I walked into the kitchen yesterday morning and found that my kids had poured boiling water over the Arm and Hammer baking soda I had put in the refrigerator. They were eating it as cream of wheat.

Are we nuts? Or is television intensely unreal? If I judged my marriage by TV's standards, I would leave today before Larry got home.

Do you realize I've never had an in-depth discussion with my husband on the subject of deodorants? We've never once endured a joint crisis of "ring around the collar." And we've never had that supreme experience of wiping the spots off the glasses before the guests arrived. How we have survived, I will never know. I'm beginning to wonder if we are aliens on this American soil.

No one in our house has ever asked why the bacon shrinks. No one has ever proven that they get raisins in every bite. I've never had a neighbor drop in to recommend a fabric softener, and a long time ago I decided that a soggy hamburger flung through a drive-up window was indeed *not* the break I deserved.

One more thing. If Mrs. Olsen walks through one more door with one more can of coffee, I just may scream. The woman herself is beginning to look "mountain grown."

Why don't those creative geniuses come up with

Usually the sun shines when I'm this prepared.

some things I really need? Like a furniture polish I drink so I can walk in a room and just blow once a week. What about magnetic socks that pair themselves in the dryer? Or cereal boxes with two prizes for people with two children?

Someone ought to come up with a better method of getting in and out of a car with an umbrella when it's pouring and you're all dressed up. I would be thrilled if someone would sell me children's shoes equipped with indestructible laces, or offer to install a self-cleaning kitchen floor.

How about a beauty shop that gives you a written guarantee that when you get home, both sides of your hair will look good at the same time? Or that sleeping on your hairdo won't ruin it!

I would like a taco that doesn't self-destruct when you take the first bite, a washing machine that screams when a black sock is circulating with the white load, a sliding glass door that doesn't show fingerprints, and a grocery cart with four wheels that roll forward.

Now those things I could really use!

I think we should all participate in a little pretending. I get great joy out of seeing my children stand on the ledge in front of the fireplace with a microphone and two strange-looking puppets. I react like you would to a nine-year-old boy in a bathrobe, a cowboy hat, and sun glasses, lip-syncing to a Mel Tillis record. And I pretend, too. Some days I pretend I feel good when I don't. Sometimes I pretend my grocery bill doesn't bother me. Once in a while I even try to pretend I want to clean the bathrooms.

Everybody pretends. If everything in life were a stark reality, we'd all be in an asylum. But there is always the danger of forgetting where pretending ends and facing life begins. And television has not helped us there.

I have sometimes wondered if my kids wished I were more like Mrs. Walton. However, when my daughter said she thought Abby from "Eight is Enough" is a neat mother, I decided a little reality was called for.

If I got up every morning and drove to a studio where I walked on a set already cleaned by someone else; where I welcomed my children who had already been fed, dressed, and run through a room where an expert put straight parts in their hair; and where I greeted a make-believe husband who had showered, eaten, and worked out his early morning kinks on someone else, I might come off a lot better than I do.

What we see is cute—good entertainment—but it is pretend stuff, folks, not reality! Reality is the program being presented by the PTA at my kids' elementary school tonight on drug abuse.

A lot of television programs are off limits in our house, for obvious reasons. But I'm not against television. We need to be entertained occasionally; we certainly need to be informed, and there are some programs that really teach us something. Just don't begin to expect your problems to be solved between commercials.

Even Christian television doesn't always show us reality. Christians have bad days, too, and they don't always grin their way through them. There are times when Christians cry, times when they want to give up.

Aren't you glad you can walk out on the front porch, look up at the vastness of the blue sky, the smattering of magnificent clouds, and the birds that no one teaches to fly—and know that God is real?

Aren't you reassured by the fact that you can stand in the anxious atmosphere of a hospital emergency room and in the peaceful throne room of God at the same time, knowing that the real Comforter has placed His everlasting arms around you?

My God is real . . . and He *is* the God of reality. His offers are not seasonal. His promises aren't "new and improved." His love doesn't come with a one-year guarantee. His constant availability doesn't depend on volume of business. His willingness to carry your burdens doesn't fall apart when you get it home.

God is our refuge and strength, a very present help in trouble (Ps. 46:1).

"I am come as a light into the world, that whosoever believes in Me should not abide in darkness" (John 12:46).

"Peace I leavo with you, My peace I give to you; not as the world gives do I give to you. Let not your heart be troubled, neither let it be afraid" (John 14:27).

Every good gift and every perfect gift is from above, and comes down from the Father of lights, with whom there is no variation or shadow of turning (James 1:17).

In these days when most people can't tell what's real and what isn't, there is no variation or shadow of turning with God. That means He doesn't change, and He doesn't turn His back on you. "Jesus Christ is the same yesterday, today, and forever" (Heb. 13:8).

We have an antique kerosene lamp sitting on our piano. We've never used it; we just look at it. Several years ago, one of my children asked me what the lamp was for. Profoundly, I answered, "To give light."

Then I heard, "Is it a pretend lamp, Mommy? Is that why it doesn't work?"

"No, it's real, honey. We just don't use it."

The next question I expected.

"Why don't we use it?"

"Because it's easier to turn on the other lights, I guess."

We have living within us the Light of the World, a real source of potential power in our lives. How often do we use it?

Somehow we think it is easier to keep trying new methods, reaching out to new concepts, clinging on to the hope that tomorrow things will all work out. After all, dealing with reality God's way might force a few changes!

But when it's all said and done, and things have fallen apart . . . when we've pretended all we can pretend, we turn to the real thing.

You can sit in front of the television with your children and point out the difference between a commercial and a good job of acting. But who's going to do the same thing for you? Who is going to walk through your home and help you see where facts are being dealt with and where self-deceit has taken over?

Only God can do that. He alone can give clear insight where we've let the fog roll in.

My dad, who is a preacher, has been on the radio most of his life. For a long time he has ended his programs with this sign-off: "Joyfully yours in the reality of Christianity, this is Louis Paul Lehman."

I used to think that was weird. But now I know he knew much more than I gave him credit for.

In fact, I think I'll steal the line—out of gratitude, of course: "Joyfully yours in the reality of Christianity, this is your daughter."

Chapter 10

Softening of
The Heart-eries

I have a wonderful friend whose name is
Phillip. He is eight years old. I met him more than six
years ago when his family began coming to the
church we attended. We all seemed to hit it off very
quickly. Phillip was close in age to our son Jason; his
sister was three years younger than our Melissa; and
Larry and I developed a strong friendship with their
mother and father after just a few hours together.

Today, Phillip's mother is my closest friend—the
kind of friend I will never replace. And even though we
now live halfway across the country from each other,
there is still a special bond between our families.

Phillip has more energy for life than any other five
people put together. If you were to pull into his
driveway after school today, he would probably greet
you from the seat of the riding lawn mower, which is
unquestionably his personal property. He can oper-
ate it with great precision, and he even hooks a
wagon on the back when the leaves need to be picked
up. He enjoys helping to fix the car or the pickup
truck that takes him and his best friend—his dad—to

94

the farm. And he shows nothing but sheer delight when he gets to drive the tractor.

Like all eight-year-old boys, his shoes are usually muddy, his trucks are often lined up on the family-room floor, and his room has a thing or two out of place.

On the other hand, he can break his own egg, cook his own breakfast, or clean up the kitchen after supper. He has a broad smile, a terrific sense of humor, and a physique that one day will be the envy of any professional football player.

But he also has isolated brain damage, which affects primarily his finer motor skills.

Catching a ball, drawing a tree, or putting a puzzle together have always been more difficult for Phillip than for most of the kids with whom he plays. But God has given him a strong will, a determined personality, and parents who are giving him every opportunity and every kind of help to see that he becomes all he can be.

His progress has been phenomenal. When I see him once or twice a year, I am genuinely excited to see new abilities, finer skills, and the good papers he has brought home from the public school he attends with the other kids in his neighborhood.

The last time I was visiting in Phillip's home, the two of us managed to sneak away for a giant banana split and some heavy conversation. We discussed his friends, the farm, his teachers, and the fact that he had passed his swimming test. I hardly got a word in edgewise, because the only time he quit talking was when the spoon was in his mouth. I looked across the table and smiled as I remembered those days when each new word added to his vocabulary was a victory.

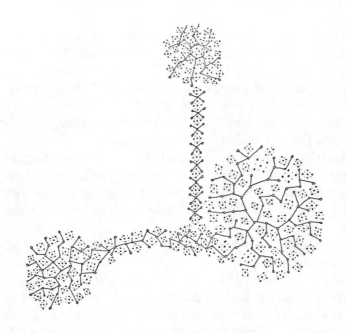

I feel all tingley inside.

I recalled in particular one time years ago, when I was in his home for several weeks. From time to time, I would spend a few minutes with Phillip working on a word or two. One day, with the help of a red balloon, we began to work on "up" and "down." We hit the balloon, and as it sailed I would say "up"; as it dropped and hit the floor I would say "down." Phillip watched intently, laughed, and continued to use his own personal vocabulary instead of the words I kept repeating.

I didn't give up. The balloon felt bruised, I'm sure, and my enthusiasm was at a low point when all of a sudden Phillip said "up." Not long after, I began to hear "down." As I wrapped my arms around him and started to cry, he beamed from ear to ear. I guess the next hour was filled with nothing but "ups" and "downs" of the best kind, and when his folks came home we ran up the stairs, balloon in hand, to show off a little. He performed proudly to the most responsive audience in the world.

There is no doubt that my friend Phillip will achieve much in his lifetime. It wouldn't surprise me if he proves medical statistics invalid and current data obsolete.

But when he has completed his education and has found his spot in life, the "ups" and "downs" will still be mine. Those two words will always remind me of my friend Phillip. He has probably forgotten my small addition to his life, but he has given me much in return. He has allowed me the privilege of being moved and stirred inside by the life of another warm human being.

I wish there were a way to describe what I mean when I say my heart has been moved. Being moved is first and most importantly an inside matter. It is an instinctive tremor amidst your feelings, a slight jolt to your emotions.

Emotions are wonderful things. They are the very breath of life to logical thoughts, the four-color process of our imagination, and the window displays of our innermost feelings.

They are those little jelly-like things that kept us awake the night before our birthday and on every Christmas Eve. They caused static and interference in various communications with our parents and covered us with cozy security when Dad sat on the side of the bed and told us how much he loved us. Emotions can make us tingle and almost glow in the dark. They can tug at our heartstrings, make our noses run, make our feet tap to the beat of the music, and produce goosebumps the instant a band plays "Stars and Stripes Forever."

When I was in college, I went through a stage I call "Hardening of the Heart-eries." I thought that if I worked at being less emotional, at being harder and colder, I wouldn't get hurt so much. I figured if I didn't get excited about anything, I wouldn't talk so much, bite off bigger projects than I could chew, or cry when a guy took me to see *The Sound of Music*.

Well, I pulled through that stage and went through a dozen more.

Today, however, I am grateful for my God-given emotions. Like everybody else, my emotions have been played with, misused a time or two, sat on, criticized, and sealed in plastic. I am pleased to announce that mine survived and, much to my delight, are fully intact as of this moment.

There is a big difference between letting your

emotions control your life and allowing your emotions to be a vital part of your life. There is also a big difference between an emotional person and a person with deep emotions. Adults have the tendency to work so hard at controlling the emotions that create difficulties that they also extinguish the enriching ones in the process. And we often call this maturity!

If that's maturity, you can have it! I'll keep my tears and my excitement and my pain, even when no one else around understands just what it was that moved me.

My family often laughs at my ability to "cry without plot." I can walk in when the television is on, at a time when the story is half over; I can sit down without any understanding of the roles or the first thirty minutes of action; and if the violins are playing and the actors are saying the right words to each other—I cry.

You can imagine what shape I'm in when I watch the whole thing! That is not an example of my deepest emotions, of course, but I no longer apologize for being easily moved.

One phrase I hear everywhere I go these days is, "I'm not shocked by anything anymore." I'm not so sure that the statement shouldn't be, "I'm not *moved* by anything any more."

We are exposed to so much, we see and hear so much that I think we sometimes find it easier to shut it all out than to face it.

Christian, you who have heard the gospel all your life, how long has it been since you've felt God tugging at your heart? How long has it been since you've stood over the bed of your healthy, sleeping child and felt the tears of gratefulness sting your eyes? Maturity doesn't belittle tenderness. Spiritual growth doesn't take place in hardened soil or unmovable granite.

Compassion, gentleness, kindness, and love are not dutiful qualities but responses of the God-centered heart. God gave us emotion just as He gave us fingers and toes and nostrils.

Don't become so hardened that you can hear the testimony of someone whose life has been changed by the message of the gospel and go untouched by God's continuing power. Don't push the tears back so often that you become proud of the fact that a child's prayer can no longer make you weep.

The prayer meetings in most of our churches are now mostly "meeting," with very little prayer. You certainly don't see many men let tears stream down their faces as they pray for their unsaved children, and it is rather out of vogue to carry a tear-stained Bible today.

> For God so loved the world that He gave His only begotten Son, that whosoever believeth in Him should not perish but have everlasting life (John 3:16).

This is by far the most well-known verse in the Bible. We've read it, even recited it, for twenty or thirty or maybe fifty years. How long has it been since you allowed it to move you?

I'm not asking you to base your salvation on feeling. Salvation is received through faith, and the assurance that I am a child of God is found in my knowledge of His love, His promises, His Word, and what *I know* He has done in my life. But I am asking how warm and responsive you are to God's heart.

We get excited about the way God answered prayer yesterday, but we become further and further removed from what He did for us through the death of His Son on the cross. The fact that He was crucified, that He bled and died for our sins, should move us as nothing else does. The fact that He arose should fill us with life and hope and anticipation.

If we can go year after year, never overwhelmed with God's love, never moved to tears because of what He has done for us—there is something wrong.

It was my privilege to take part in the musical and dramatic presentation of the cantata *No Greater Love* some years ago. It was written to be performed during the Easter season; it covers the life, death, and resurrection of Christ.

The lead male role was played by one of the finest Christian men I have ever met—Gary Moore. In my estimation he has one of the greatest voices in the field of Christian music today, and he combines that dedicated talent with a sensitive spirit and a genuine love for his Lord.

During the performances of this production, the stage was blacked out during the Crucifixion scene. All that could be seen was the outline of a cross as we sat there in total darkness. Nothing broke the silence of those moments but the penetrating thuds of nails being driven into wood. The thunder crashed and the lightning flashed streaks of death as a hush lay like a blanket over the audience.

When the music began quietly, with the choir singing, "There is no greater love," the stage lights would slowly come up. Each time I would see Gary Moore, dressed in full biblical costume, weeping. It didn't make any difference that we'd rehearsed it many times, or that he knew a man backstage was pounding the stakes. Each time he was moved all over again by the magnitude of God's love—by the awesomeness of the fact that Christ died for him. I seldom see that kind of emotion among Christians.

Too many of us who have been in church all our lives have become spiritually numb. We are no longer moved to sheer delight by thinking about our salvation; we seldom feel the new life that comes from the cleansing power of God's total forgiveness. It's been a long time since we've experienced that emotion of being filled to overflowing with gratefulness to God for the unspeakable gift of His Son.

I want always to be movable inside. I want to cry for joy when Phillip gives his first speech in front of the student body. I want to spill over with emotion when I hear Gary Moore sing about the return of Christ the King. And I want to be able to weep with gratefulness when I think of what God has done in my life.

My prayer is that God will use my emotions—if for nothing else—to keep me tender toward Him.

Chapter 11

I'm Caught in a Web, And I'm the Spider

As a preacher's kid, I have sat through a lot of prayer meetings. In fact, I've slept through a few. Once I was awakened by a giggling friend who informed me that I had disturbed everyone in the room by snoring!

Over the years, I guess I've heard people pray for just about everything in just about every situation. I remember the day the president of my Christian high school prayed about gnats. The weather was hot and humid, and the pests were on the rampage. He simply looked toward heaven and asked the Lord to get the gnats out of our way so we could study.

I remember the day our kids prayed for a baby brother or sister, and I prayed simultaneously, "Not me, Lord, please, not me!"

I have heard people pray for every missionary they have ever known—by name and country.

I have heard one person pray for rain and another pray for continued sunshine, all in the same five minutes.

I have listened to short prayers, long prayers, and "I-can-outdo-you" prayers.

I have endured prayers to impress an audience and been moved by prayers that expressed one's needs.

I have heard quiet prayers that, I'm sure, literally shattered the gates of heaven.

I have heard prayers to the King of Kings and prayers to the "friend that sticketh closer than a brother."

I have heard prayers of intimate conversation and prayers of exuberant worship.

Prayers come in all sizes and moods and intensities. An individual's prayer is as unique as the creature it comes from. And prayer can vary with each situation.

My mother has prayed many nights on my behalf; but one night in particular she prayed for me and my unborn child, because both of us were in deep trouble. She prayed earnestly in that hospital waiting room, a candy bar in one hand and a cup of coffee in the other.

I sat in a dirty little house on a Sunday morning in Manila, where some forty people had squeezed into a room hardly big enough for ten. Amidst the dogs and chickens and more flies than you see at a church picnic, the people prayed in a language I didn't understand. And there were no distractions from the real presence of God in that place.

Today, as you're reading this, there are people praying for a million dollars to save a business. There are others praying for twenty dollars to feed their children.

Some people are praying for a new car, and others are praying for shoes to cover their feet. Children are praying for parents. Parents are praying for children. And some folks are praying for someone they have prayed for every day for years. Some people are praying in the midst of a crisis. Some are thanking God for seeing them through a time of trouble. Some are rejoicing, and some are pleading for relief in their sorrow.

What are you praying for?

You know, one thing has always puzzled me. In all the prayers I have heard I have never heard anyone pray for self-discipline. Think about it. How many things in your day-to-day life would change and improve if you had more discipline?

For one thing, we would probably be more consistent in starting our day with the Lord—and that alone would make a big difference. Praying for self-discipline would give us a much better chance of making it past the second day of our thirty-day exercise plan, the third day of our diet, and the fourth day of our correspondence course.

I have had the privilege of learning a lot about the efforts and rewards of self-discipline, especially in the area of losing weight. I weighed 340 pounds, and through four years of struggling, not only with my sugar addiction but with my ability to let God change my life, I learned a great deal.

Today I am 217 pounds lighter, and *God knows I won't be fat again.*

I do count that experience a privilege, because the interesting thing about self-discipline is that as you begin to develop it in one area of your life, it spills over into other untidy areas as well. Consequently, my eating habits are not the only things that have been brought under control.

105

And today, I still can't think of many of my everyday struggles that couldn't be handled if I had the discipline to do what I know I should do and could do.

A few years ago, I decided to start going back to the Conservatory of Music to continue my piano studies. It sounds impressive, but it didn't last long. Everyone understood when I told them I found it difficult to practice twelve hours a week with two small children in the house. But I could have done it had I really disciplined myself. I could tell you I didn't feel at the time it was God's will for me to continue—but that's not true. The fact is, I wasn't willing to discipline myself.

My dad told me something when I was growing up that is worth repeating: "For every ounce of talent, there must be an ounce of self-discipline, or the talent God gave you isn't worth much."

We want the Lord to give us talent. But we also want Him to develop the talent for us.

God has given each of us gifts—talents to do something for Him. But we must ask Him to help us develop these talents so we can use them effectively. If we don't have any self-discipline in our lives, we won't accomplish anything.

The kitchen floor doesn't shine unless we scrub and wax it. And all the good intentions in the world cannot replace the bucket, the mop, and the reality that we have to sweat if we want to be pleased with the outcome.

My paternal grandmother was a brilliant woman—Florence Esther Genevieve Moline Lehman by name (and she loved to use the whole thing). She could write, act, direct a hundred people in an original pageant, and make her own hats. She was an articulate and dramatic speaker, a natural artist, and she could prepare a smorgasbord that would stretch clear out of the dining room.

The sad thing is that she did all these things only when the pressure was on, and then she seemed to accomplish only what she absolutely had to.

Florence was fifty-four when I was born, and when I was three my grandfather died. At fifty-seven, this gifted lady was left with abundant talent, unlimited potential, and a total lack of self-discipline. Publishing houses wanted her to write. She had the opportunity to become a sought-after speaker. She had all the background and knowledge to become an effective Bible teacher. She could have pioneered the field of Christian drama. She was healthy, strong, imaginative, and had the financial freedom to choose any area of productivity.

But instead, for twenty-six years—more than a quarter of a century—she chose to do nothing. During the years I knew her she became more and more of a recluse, finally exercising her imagination only through talking to and putting on plays with her collection of Hummel figurines. The little porcelain people eventually became her only friends.

Her life consisted of going to the grocery store once a week, watching television, and reading through one cookbook after another.

I found her fascinating. She talked of circuses and ice capades, and described in minute detail the imaginary bugs on the wall who all wore undershirts. She showed me stacks of beautiful fabrics that would have made gorgeous hats and stunning outfits. She had piles of unopened patterns, files of untried recipes, and a mind full of brilliant ideas and captivating stories. She was daring in concept, nonconforming in style, and gave life to everything she described.

But the stories never got from her mind onto paper. The fabrics were never used. And her Hummels were the only recipients of her great wit and superb mental strategy.

She died at eighty-three, weighing close to three hundred pounds, never having found the discipline to do anything with the marvelous gifts God had given her.

I have every human tendency to be just like her. I, too, find it difficult to produce if I'm not under pressure. I usually end up doing only what I feel I *have* to do. So many of my ideas go untried. So many stories go unwritten. And seldom do I feel I've been disciplined enough to work at my maximum capacity. But for the help of God, I would end up just like my grandmother.

That's why the prayer for self-discipline seems so vitally important to me. I don't want to waste my life and my God-given abilities.

In Psalms 19:13, David prayed: "Keep back thy servant also from presumptuous sins; let them not have dominion over me." Presumptuous sin is presuming that God is going to do for us what He has given us the strength to do. He wouldn't have given us abilities if He hadn't intended for us to accomplish something.

And those of us who sit with unused and undeveloped talents, waiting for the Lord to miraculously use us, never willing to exercise self-discipline, will never know the fullness of what God meant us to be.

Of course, when we pray for self-discipline we must remember that God gives it only through faithful, consistent, "stick-to-it-iveness" made strong by the power of His life in ours.

I urge you to make a list of all the things you have been meaning to do, feel you can't do, and wish you could make yourself do. Then see how many of them are tied to the lack of self-discipline.

I've been able to scratch a few off my list. Each time I eliminate one, I am encouraged to go on to the next. As I tackle each new sloppy segment of my life, I know I'm in for some hours of concentration, or the pain of breaking some bad habits, or the consistency of a bitter attitude. But I am eager to know what God can do with a disciplined life.

Once our own lives approach some semblance of order, the question then becomes, how do you teach the importance of self-discipline to your children? It's one of the qualities I want them to have and take with them when they leave our home to build their future.

You can show them that the stove is hot, that a knife is sharp, or that flies get into the kitchen when they leave the back door open. They can see their muddy footprints on the living-room rug, they can feel your disappointment when they have lied; but how do you help them understand something so internally motivated as self-discipline?

They understand forced discipline, but that comes from without, not from within. I can make them do things for twenty years, but if they never discover the value of making *themselves* do things, they will always just "get by."

I can see the cereal companies aren't going to help me; they still haven't come up with a self-discipline-

I get angry about being caught in the web . . .
forgetting that I'm the spider!

fortified breakfast yum-yum. The vitamin companies still haven't put self-discipline in capsule form. The T-shirt marketing experts feel there is little demand for an iron-on patch that says, "S.D. is my game."

I have thought, I have prayed, and I have brought all my creative powers to their peak, but I must tell you I have come up with only two ways that children learn self-discipline. Neither way sounds revolutionary, but I still can't run away from them.

(1) Most of our kids are going to learn one third of whatever self-discipline they learn the hard way. They're going to fail a few times, lose a few times, or be passed up for a lead part or a good job. They're going to learn, as all of us do, that the winners are those who worked harder, did more than they had to, and were willing to stick with it when everyone else quit. They also will learn that they have a choice to either remain as they are or get to work.

(2) The other two-thirds of their self-discipline, if they have it, will come from their parents. It won't result, for the most part, from what we say—but from what we are. Do our children see the value of self-discipline by the difference it makes in our lives?

Perhaps they come home every day to a mother sitting in front of the TV set. Maybe they hear us make promises we never keep. They may occasionally hear us beg out of projects halfway through because we are not willing to work that hard. Do they see the pile of books we are always going to read? Are they tired of being told that a certain night of the week will be kept for them and realizing it never works out? Are we continually late because we can't discipline ourselves to start early enough?

Then we shouldn't preach self-discipline or wonder why our capable children don't realize how important it is to do their best in school.

Don't misunderstand me. No one is totally self-disciplined, and I'm not saying we have to score nine out of ten before we can impart anything to our kids. We just need to be sure they are aware we are working at it.

Be honest with your kids about *your* need for self-discipline in certain areas of *your* life. Show them a list of two or three things you're working on, and ask them to check your progress occasionally and give you any suggestions they may have. Let them hear you pray for self-discipline in the specific project you're working on. Then make sure you share with them the rewards of your perseverance.

If they begin to see the value of your efforts, God's ability to help you, and the way those changes not only affect your life but theirs as well, an inside impression will begin to appear.

They may even bring you their list and ask for your encouragement! At that point you have my permission to look heavenward and say, "This is great stuff, Lord. I've improved, and so has the kid in the football jersey and the space helmet. Thanks for your help . . . again."

A passage from Paul's first Letter to the church in Corinth always excites me and is very applicable to this subject:

In a race, everyone runs but only one person gets

first prize. So run your race to win. To win the contest you must deny yourselves many things that would keep you from doing your best. An athlete goes to all this trouble just to win a blue ribbon or a silver cup, but we do it for a heavenly reward that never disappears. So I run straight to the goal with purpose in every step. I fight to win. I'm not just shadow-boxing or playing around. Like an athlete I punish my body, treating it roughly, training it to do what it should, not what it wants to. Otherwise I fear that after enlisting others for the race, I myself might be declared unfit and ordered to stand aside" (1 Cor. 9:24–27, TLB).

I have a feeling that if Paul were scheduled to speak tonight, and if he chose to use the above passage as part of his speech, the topic just might be self-discipline.

Chapter 12

Liberated Ladies —
Are You Listening?

It was a cold, rainy night. Larry and I were getting ready to go to a fancy dinner at a downtown hotel.

He was running late, as usual. He had already been in the bathroom an hour, but he was still complaining that his hair wouldn't go right, and he had retied his tie at least a dozen times.

I had gone after the baby-sitter, and the traffic was awful. Looking at my watch, I realized that with this weather we'd never make it on time, so I told him I'd keep the car running so it would be warm when he got in.

On my way to the garage I stumbled over three pairs of tennis shoes he had had all day to put away. I noticed at a glance that he hadn't swept the kitchen floor either. Wondering what he does with all his time, I got into the car, turned on the heater, and twiddled my thumbs for another three minutes.

All the way downtown in the blinding rain, I kept both eyes glued to the highway to keep us out of danger, while Larry, completely oblivious to the weather, kept asking me to glance over at him to see if he looked all right. He wanted to know if his tie tack was straight . . . if he'd chosen the right belt . . . and what I thought of the new shoes he'd gotten on sale last week.

I nodded yes to everything and managed to pull up to the hotel just seven minutes late. I let Larry out under the canopy, drove across the street, and parked the car—at which time I discovered he had carried the umbrella into the house with the groceries and forgotten to put it back. My only choice was to pull my coat around me and make a run for it. My open-toe shoes were incompatible with the puddles, and I had a close call with a spray of muddy water from a passing car. But I managed to get across the street and through the revolving doors unharmed.

My toes were wet, my dress a little spotted, and my hair slightly wind-blown, but I was glad I had been able to get Larry right up to the door. He looked terrific—and not a hair out of place. We found the room where the dinner was being held, and soon we were meeting other guests and having a wonderful time.

Larry almost forgot to let me pull the chair out for him at the table, and I had trouble finding a place to hang his coat. But other than that the evening was pleasant and uninterrupted. After the banquet and the program, we had coffee downstairs with three other couples. As usual, the women argued about who was going to pick up the tab, but I finally outsmarted the others and had the waitress bring the bill directly to me.

When we got back out to the lobby we discovered it was still raining, so we left the gentlemen inside the

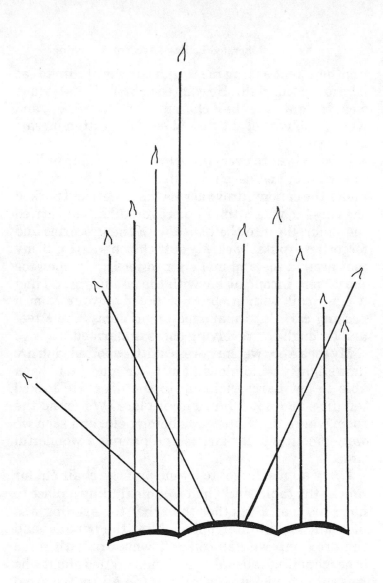

Darling, do you think the wedding candles are trying to tell us something?

front door where it was warm, and the four of us dashed in different directions to get the cars.

After paying the parking ticket that I had forgotten to have stamped, I turned the key and discovered my battery was dead. I had to have one of the other women, who fortunately had parked in the same lot, give me a hand by connecting our batteries with her jumper cables. It started right away, but by that time I was soaked. I pulled up under the canopy where my dry, smiling husband was waiting. I went around and opened the door, motioning for him to come and get in. Of course, he wanted to know what had taken me so long, and when he realized how soaked I was, he sat close to the door so his suit wouldn't get wet.

All the way home, he couldn't talk about anything except how I was going to catch cold . . . how he wished he had left that old towel in the car so I could dry my hair . . . and wasn't that an awful outfit the man at our table was wearing.

Soon we reached the refuge of our garage. He went into the house, sent the baby-sitter out (telling her, I'm sure, not to be alarmed by the way I looked), and I took her home. When I returned he was upstairs, already in his pajamas and in the bathroom. I locked the doors, turned out the lights, picked up the three pairs of tennis shoes, and set them on the kitchen counter so he'd be sure to see them in the morning. I walked slowly up the stairs. As I looked at my soggy dress that had just come from the cleaners and realized how much money the outing had cost, I heard Larry yell from the other room, "Wasn't that a marvelous evening?"

—The End—

Yes, it's just a story. The roles, of course, have been reversed. It was just my way of telling you how much I like being a woman, and keeping my hair dry and my toes warm.

I suppose there are groups here and there who would like to know if I've kept detailed records to see if Larry has opened enough doors, found enough canopies, and hung up enough coats to offset the loads of laundry I've done and the socks I've matched.

I'll tell you, I'm sick and tired of pink and blue balance sheets. Whatever happened to grace and forbearance? Love still remains the best motivation in the world, and it seems to be an unbeatable equalizer in marriage.

If we keep promoting the idea that men and women have totally equal roles, we're going to have one awful mess. Take our house, for example. Larry would be doing half of the home decorating. I would be responsible for fixing half of the bicycle chains and half of the broken "what-cha-ma-call-its" that keep the water from squirting out of the wrong place. Larry would be keeping the closets clean, and I would be building the fires with the damper closed. Within three months, the county would have to come out and shut us down.

Now, I feel I probably have the intelligence to learn how to do all the things my husband does—and vice versa. But I don't want to be mannish. I like the arrangement the way it is. He has his strong points and I have mine—and when we combine them everything gets done, and gets done well.

I don't like the fact that today all women are being put into one of two categories:

(1) The whiney, helpless woman who sits in a silk dressing gown and paints her fingernails every morning from nine to ten. Her schedule is limited to lunch with the girls, tennis twice a week, and walking around on her husband's arm. She has no real intelligence, no individual interests, and no goals other than to look pretty and dress in the latest fashion.

(2) The assertive woman who is out there fighting for her rights. She wants to pay for her husband's meal, open her own doors, and drive an eighteen-wheeler. She has a pushy personality, no shared interests, and no goal other than to prove that anything a man can do she can do better.

Whatever happened to the rest of us? There's a whole category missing here. We are not very newsworthy. We're not revolutionary enough for the magazines, and we make dull film footage. But we happen to be one of the most positive and valuable assets this country has. We are women who love being what we are!

I have no desire to be treated like a man, to act like a man, or to assume the role of a man. I love being helped across the street. I appreciate staying under canopies when it rains, and I like having daisies pushed at me when my husband walks in the back door.

I don't resent the fact that I do the cleaning and the laundry and the cooking, and I don't want to exchange these jobs for the opportunity to build a highway or drive a truck. I like to smell pretty, and I love to be told I look breathtaking. Furthermore, it is possible to work full time, have a great deal of intelligence, have goals and interests, and still be a woman through and through. It is possible for me to carry the garbage can to the end of the driveway and still have my nails painted. It is possible for a feminine, ladylike person to be a good and submissive helpmate.

I can wear a beautiful negligee at night and go to work in the morning to help pay the bills, if that is what helps my family most. I can kiss a skinned knee, serve Kool-Aid to the kids in the neighborhood, rub my husband's back, and work on my own projects without feeling threatened or unable to express myself.

As a Christian, I know that God created women to be women. He gave us a unique makeup, different from but complementary to men. We are not the same, and no matter how hard the world tries to change that, we never will be. God said the man is to be head of the household; he is to protect his wife and children; he is responsible for his family. Now, I admit that Christian men don't always meet God's qualifications, but God still intended for them to be men.

And just what is a Christian woman? Today, she is many things—a car pool driver . . . a cub scout leader . . . a Sunday school teacher . . . a private tutor . . . and sometimes a full-time employee. But a Christian woman shouldn't be appreciated only for what she *does,* but for what she *is.* The world doesn't understand this, because the progress of women today is being calculated by the progress of their *careers* and not the development of their *characters*.

The Book of Proverbs contains a partial description of a Christian woman.

> She is a woman of strength and dignity, and has no fear of old age. When she speaks, her words are wise, and kindness is the rule for everything she says. She watches carefully all that goes on throughout her household and is never lazy. Her children stand and bless her; so does her husband. He praises her with these words: "There are many fine women in the world, but you are the best of them all!" Charm can be deceptive, and beauty doesn't last, but a woman who fears and reverences God shall be greatly praised (31:25–30, TLB).

What a high calling! What a privilege! The effectiveness of a Christian woman who is all she should be in Christ is greater than the strongest of all the potential outcomes of the ERA. The high calling of a Christian woman in this day presents an opportunity for more strength, more challenge, and more character than any career I can think of.

Ours is a great legacy. I believe Christian women are the greatest source of prayer in this country today. I am convinced that Christian mothers are the ones hanging tight to a biblical morality. I know that Christian wives can help to lower the divorce rate of this nation.

We are not namby-pambies. We are women who like what we are and have a job to do. We are in a position of honor and responsibility. And I am ready to hear a few people say so!

It doesn't take any wisdom, intelligence, or strength to walk away from responsibility, difficulty, financial instability, or a bunch of things you don't like. Anyone can do that. It does take a special strength and a deep commitment to see it through . . . to stick with your marriage and make it work . . . to use your God-given abilities and still assume your responsibilities.

I believe Christian women have the resources to bring about a real change in society . . . a change back to what God intended us to be. And when I say Christian woman, I don't mean a stiff, plain, sexless, spiritual giant. I mean a woman who is alive and radiant and alluring to the man she loves.

Tell your husband how you appreciate the little things he does for you. Stick a note in his lunch bag—"I love you. Your bologna sandwich is sealed with a kiss." Be feminine; snuggle up; put your cold feet on his back. You are a woman. Don't be ashamed of it!

I'm fed up with chair*persons* and sales *persons* and mail*persons*. The next time you're surveyed in a shopping mall and they ask you your occupation, tell them you're working in the greatest position in the world, with all the potential and challenge that could be offered to any human being. Tell them you are a woman with the future of becoming all that God intended you to be. It's a lofty position, indeed!

Chapter 13

A Bag of Surprises

My husband threw a surprise birthday party for me once, and it was really a surprise—not one I had to fake! I was in bed, asleep. At 12:30 A.M. the telephone rang. I threw one heavy arm over the side of the bed, grabbed the receiver, and heard my folks on the other end. Now admittedly, it was officially December 1, but I did think they were jumping the gun a bit. I chatted through the fog in my mind, thanked them rather insincerely for remembering, and hung up.

I was just about asleep again when the doorbell rang. I kicked Larry and told him to go and see who could be at the door at that hour. A minute later he came running into the bedroom, gave me an emergency-type reason to follow him (which seemed logical to me at the time), and insisted I grab my robe.

I rushed down the hall—half numb—opened the door like any dumbbell would, and found forty-three people with paper hats and whistles standing on our front porch and covering our front lawn . . . singing the early morning version of that old familiar tune, "Happy Birthday."

Later I found out that my folks had called to cover the sounds of the fleet parking and the car doors slamming. In the meantime, there I was—decked out in enormous pink rollers, no makeup at all, wearing my oldest nightgown and the tackiest robe I owned—facing all my friends.

What could I do? Nothing! They'd all seen me, so there wasn't much use in trying to better my appearance. I simply stood back, and they all marched into my living room. Paper plates and cups, a cake with candles, and gallons of ice cream seemed to appear from nowhere.

What a great party that was! I will always wonder how people conned their baby-sitters into reporting for work at midnight.

A surprise is something you don't expect, and there have been lots of them in my life. However, they are not very often as terrific as the one my husband dreamed up.

Just today, I allowed fifteen minutes to get to the soccer field and met thirty minutes' worth of traffic. Surprise! I went to the beauty shop yesterday so I would look better and left looking you-know-what. I went to the dentist for a routine checkup and found that I need a thousand dollars' worth of reconstruction done.

We moved into a house shaded by lots of trees and then found out that the leaves fall off. I bought a new coffee table and, much to my surprise, discovered that coffee stains that one just like it does all the other tables in the house. I brought home two perfect babies, but have since been told they need shots, lots of individual care, and braces. If I knew ahead of time all the surprises that were going to enter into my day's activities, some days I'd never get out of bed!

God also surprises me from time to time with the mysterious ways He works in my life. I'm surprised at how I'm turning out. I like what I see. I'm impressed more with the potential of my future than with its uncertainty. I am surprised at how my values have changed and how many adjustments I've made. I'm even surprised I'm still in one piece.

But what really surprises me is how God has chosen to teach me what I've learned. I expected Him to use a crisis to teach me to trust Him; instead, He has used daily hassles. I waited a long time for God to punish me for the awful things I had done in my life, and He surprised me with His total forgiveness.

When I gave the pieces of my broken life to Christ in August of 1964, I was sincerely willing to give Him the opportunity to do with me what He could. But I must admit my faith was weak; after all, what I turned over to Him was quite a mess.

Have I ever been surprised!

I have a wonderful husband, two terrific kids, a ministry, a second book just about written (if I can stay awake long enough) . . . and a dusty house.

I'm so grateful for the unexpected goodness of God. And I'm looking forward to the surprises of tomorrow, wondering how He's going to teach me the next thing I need to learn. I want to learn; I want to be where His action is. I want to experience the spectaculars of God.

There is a part of me that has never changed—the part that makes me buy tickets to the ice capades . . . that makes me love the circus. That part of me loves eccentric people ... is stimulated by overachievers ... is motivated by ideas that are new and creative and have never been tried before.

I have been pleasantly surprised to see that God's world is action-packed, shown in full color, and encourages the creativity of His children.

One of the things I enjoy is a parade. I would love to go to the Rose Bowl parade and sit in the reviewers' box. I would stand with the passing of each American flag, mark time with each band that marched in front of me, and wave back at each celebrity and costumed character. I would be amazed at the number of flowers on each float, awed by the variety of natural color, and fascinated by how the float drivers could ever see.

But you know what I'd like to do even more? March *in* the parade. That way I wouldn't miss the hustle-bustle of all those hundreds of participants lining up. I would find out what they do when a float breaks down, or when the Rose Bowl Queen can't hold her arm up to wave any longer. I would see the faces of all the children along the way, meet the people who stayed up all night and put the last rose petals on Mickey Mouse's nose, and get to be right in the midst of five tubas, ten trombones, twenty clarinets, and three tiny piccolos. Most importantly, I would be able to see where we'd been and where we were going, and learn a lot along the route ... all at the same time.

In our Christian lives, we choose either to be spectators or to march in the parade.

The spectator watches everyone else. What he sees looks effortless because he sees nothing but end results. He is satisfied to stay in one place—waving at all the right people and occasionally standing up for what he believes, when everyone is watching. He is impressed by what he sees and hears from time to time, but usually chooses to get up and go home— never really discovering anything that will alter his plans to be a spectator next year as well. There is very little difference in where he was when he became a Christian and where he is now. In his view, there is no place to go except to heaven someday. *It is the spectator who permits the spiritual giants to thrive.*

Those who choose to march in the parade very quickly pass the spectators by. They are willing to put forth the effort God requires of His faithful servants. They want to be where God is working and where people are busy pointing others to Jesus Christ. The one who is willing to walk the route knows that standing still is never what God intended for us.

The Christian life is designed to get better and better as we move further along. The one who walks with God on a day-to-day basis receives great blessings and encouragement from being able to look and see how far he's come with God's help. And the future not only holds the promise of eternal life; it holds the potential of spiritual growth and a closer walk with the Lord. When the leader is Christ, I'd much rather follow than watch.

We have a risen Savior. He wants for us the fullness of life. He wants to surprise us by giving us all that we need to keep marching.

We are pressed on every side by troubles, but not crushed and broken. We are perplexed because we don't know why things happen as they do, but we don't give up and quit. We are hunted down, but God never abandons us. We get knocked down, but we get up again and keep going. These bodies of ours are constantly facing death just as Jesus did; so it is clear to all that it is only the living Christ within who keeps us safe (2 Cor. 4:8–10, TLB).

Get up; get your uniform on. Shine! Pull that rusted talent out of the closet and polish it up. There's a band of committed Christians coming by. You're not going to let them pass you by again, are you? Exercise those promises God has given you. Be hospitable. Stretch that faith you talk about. Feel it. Face the fact that you've been a passive spectator way too long—that it's time to get on with the procession.

And by the way, don't be surprised when God does something wonderful through you. That's no surprise—it's a promise!

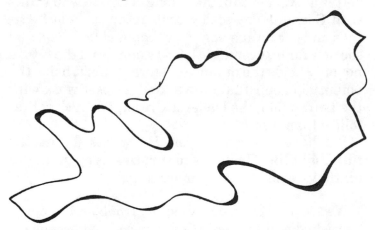

You will never know where this piece fits. . . I'm hiding the rest of the puzzle.